All proceeds from the sale of this book and associated speaking engagements will be donated to Edwards Center, a nonprofit organization providing residential and vocational services to adults with developmental disabilities (www.edwardscenter.org).

Praise for 10 Steps

"Galen Pearl has written a book that should be required reading for all attending the University of Life. She has written *10 Steps to Finding Your Happy Place (and Staying There)* with her heart in one hand and her uncommon wisdom in the other. Her prose is beautifully written, carrying the reader along as she hands us gem after gem.

Warning to any reader who picks up this book: You will likely not ever be the same again."

—KEN WERT, AUTHOR OF *A WALK THOUGH HAPPINESS*

10 Steps is a bounty of happiness tips and insightful wisdom shared through friendly, engaging stories, illustrative quotes, and simple to apply changes. You will find it hard to keep yourself from smiling as you read through this enjoyable guide. Indeed, happiness may unsuspectedly sneak right in.

—SANDRA PAWULA, ALWAYSWELLWITHIN. COM

10 Steps *to* Finding Your
Happy Place
(and Staying There)

GALEN PEARL

10 Steps to Finding You Happy Place (And Staying There)

Still Creek Press, Portland 97232

Cover image by Susan E. Inman
Author photos by Allegra Villella
Editing and production by Indigo Editing & Publications

The body text for this book is Fanwood, by Barry Schwartz.

Printed in the United States of America
21 20 19 18 17 16 15 14 13 12   1 2 3 4 5

ISBN: 978-0-9858462-0-6
Library of Congress Control Number: 2012943401

To Todd, who found the part that looked like me

Contents

Introduction   15
  Ring, Ring—Your Life Is Calling   17
  Happiness Is the Way   19

Step 1: Give Yourself Permission to Be Happy   21
  Getting Our Happiness Bearings   23
  Starter Habits   25
  Fun Is Good!   27
  Our Greatest Gift   29
  Wow   32
  Shadow Beliefs   34
  Out of the Shadows   37
  Pushing the River   40
  Life Is a Lover   42
  Dropping Our Stories   44
  Reality Check   46
  Powerful Beyond Measure   48
  The Person of Yes   50
  Show Me the Miracles!   52
  The Power to Choose   55

Step 2: Decide if You Want to Be Right or Happy   57
  I'm Right—So What!   59
  One Hand Clapping   61
  Beyond Right and Wrong   63
  A Problem Solver's Problem   65
  Nice Idea, But...   67
  The Curiosity of Not Knowing   69
  No One Wins in Court   71

The Way of No Way   73

No Right Way   75

Be Water   77

What I Know for Sure   79

Silence Is Golden   81

The Mask of Happiness   83

When Right Is Happy   85

Step 3: Give Up the Delusion of Control   89

Man Plans, God Laughs   91

The Wisdom to Know the Difference   93

The Courage to Change the Things I Can   94

It Is Not So   97

Not Doing What Fear Tells Us to Do   99

Night of the Skunk   101

Word of the Year 2011   103

Let It Go, Crow!   105

Roger That, Sparky!   107

As It Is   109

Bloom Where You're Planted   112

Grace Under Fire   114

The Doors of Change   116

Step 4: Feel Your Feelings   119

Nice to Meet You   121

Owning Our Feelings   123

Mad/Sad/Glad Game   125

The Book I Cannot Write   127

Inviting the Demons to Tea   129

Which Wolf Are You Going to Feed?   131

Transforming Our Feelings   134

I Love a Parade!   136
Cradling Our Feelings   138
Sabaay   141
Embrace the Tiger   143
Seasonal Yin Yang   146
The Joy of Sadness, the Sadness of Joy   148

Step 5: Make Haste to Be Kind   149
    Heart Hospitality   151
    That Man Might Be Jesus!   153
    What Are You Writing in Your Book?   155
    The Kindness Game   157
    Kindness Pays   159
    Make Someone's Day!   161
    Speaking the Blessing   164
    Speak Wisely   166
    It's Not About You   168
    A Few Leaves   170
    Put Your Oxygen Mask on First   172
    Mi Casa Es Su Casa   174
    New Best Friend   176
    Fake-It-Till-You-Make-It Kindness   178
    The Kindness of Strangers   180

Step 6: Judge Not   183
    Here Comes the Judge   185
    Spinning Straw into Gold   187
    Complaint-Free Challenge   189
    Expecting Ponies   191
    I Have To vs. I Get To   193
    Family Habits   195

Another's Moccasins   197
Joy with the Morning   199
Mirror, Mirror on the Wall   201
What Do Real Americans Look Like?   203
Judging Aziza   205
Who Is a Terrorist?   208
There Is No "Them"   211
The Perfection of Imperfection   214
First Date   216
From Victim to Victor   218

Step 7: Practice Compassion   221
  So Generous   223
  Who Are Your People?   225
  Mushroom Experience   227
  Calling for Love   229
  Practicing Compassion   231
  It's Oneness, Beloved   233
  Kuan Yin Calling   235
  Mary Was a Real Mother   237
  Finding Love   239
  How We See Ourselves   240
  The Best We Can   242
  Guided Tour   244
  In the Softness   246

Step 8: Forgive Everyone   249
  The F Word   251
  A Child Will Lead Them   253
  From the Ashes   255
  Righteous Unforgiveness   257

God Bless that Ol' @#&! 260

Dog Is *God* Spelled Backward 262

Giving by Asking 264

Forgiveness Sometimes Just Happens 266

The Unkindest Cut 268

Radical Forgiveness 271

For Today, Newly Bright 275

Forgiveness, the Final Frontier 277

Step 9: Develop an Attitude of Gratitude 281

An Ordinary Day 283

Voices in the Sea 285

I'm Grateful for That! 288

On the Lookout for Love 290

T-Shirt Wisdom 292

Christmas Spiders 294

My Plan B Family 296

Be Glad in It 299

Who Found That Parking Place? 302

I Love My Life! 304

Our Treasurest Place 306

Butterfly Time 307

Contentment: Priceless 310

Step 10: Be Here Now 313

You Are Here 315

The Good Old Days 317

Eternity in a Dewdrop 319

The Hidden Life of Minds 321

Awake! 323

Game Change 325

Ecstasy in the Laundry   328
Common Senses   330
Training Our Mind Puppy   332
You Have to Be Present to Win   334
Love Your Death   336
Be Amazed!   338
Falling into Now   339

The 11th Step: You Can Go Home Again   341
    Whither to Now, O Beloved?   343

Further Reading   345

About the Author   351

Introduction

Risk

And then the day came,
when the risk
to remain tight
in a bud
was more painful
than the risk
it took
to Blossom.

—ANAÏS NIN

Ring, Ring—Your Life Is Calling

My daughter's boyfriend was visiting. He is a monster football player. Believe me, you do not want to be holding the football when this guy is running toward you (although if you see him with his helmet off, you notice the dimples and he looks more cuddly than intimidating). I walked through the living room where they were sitting on the couch. His shoulders were slumped, and he had the most forlorn expression on his face. My daughter was sitting next to him patting his back. He looked so sad that I paused mid-stride, wondering whether I should say something. My daughter looked up at me, her brows furrowed with concern, and said softly, "Emanuel is looking for his happy place."

I walked on through the room, trying not to laugh at the thought of this tough guy looking for his happy place. But I couldn't stop thinking about the phrase. We've all been there, looking for our happy place. Maybe you are there now. As I contemplated Emanuel's search, I realized, with some sense of relief and gratitude, that I have found my happy place, and that I live in it most of the time.

I haven't always lived here. My journey started, as the poem suggests, with pain—in my case, physical pain. The pain started on a beautiful day in May. It began as slight twinges in the area of my solar plexus. Over the course of the afternoon, the twinges became stabs. I had never had heartburn, but I thought perhaps that was what I was experiencing. I was very uncomfortable, but not alarmed. As day turned into night, and it became too late to call my doctor, the pain got down to business. I was doubled over moaning, with dancing devils brandishing fiery hot pokers in my midsection, when I finally crawled to a phone and called a friend to take me to the emergency room.

The doctor in the emergency room asked me to rate the pain on a scale of one to ten, with ten being childbirth. Without hesitation and without ever having given birth, I gasped, "Twelve!" I briefly wondered how the doctor would describe ten to a man, but the pain yanked me back to the exam room.

The initial diagnosis was gallstones, but tests revealed none. Ulcer? Nope. They drugged me into blessed oblivion and sent me home with instructions for follow-up tests. By the next morning, I intuitively knew, and I was right, that the tests would reveal nothing. I understood that this was my wake-up call from life.

In case I missed the point, or was tempted to ignore it, I ended up in the hospital again ten days later, a horribly real déjà vu—life was urgently screaming at me that my choice to remain tight in a bud was going to become excruciatingly more painful than would making fundamental changes in my life. Lying in the emergency room a second time, I vowed to risk everything to blossom.

This book is about how I found my happy place. My hope is that it might help you find your happy place, too.

I am no prophet or guru. I am no expert. I am a beginner. Always.

*In the beginner's mind there are many possibilities,
but in the expert's there are few.*
—Shunryu Suzuki-roshi

Happiness Is the Way

There is no way to happiness. Happiness is the way.
–Thich Nhat Hanh

If someone asked us if we want to be happy, most of us would say yes. What we mean by this is not necessarily that we want to feel giddily euphoric all the time. What we mean is that we want a deep, abiding sense of joy in our lives. We are lousy predictors of what will actually make us happy. Many of us hold our happiness hostage to some future circumstances: *I'll be happy when I get a job, when I lose weight, when my kids shape up, when I meet the right person, when I move, when I get my book published, when the weather changes, when I take that trip I've always wanted, when I win the lottery.*

However, even if you got every single wish on your "when" list, it would account for at most only 10 percent of your overall happiness. Only 10 percent! Psychologist Sonja Lyubomirsky has found that besides our basic genetic temperament, which establishes our happiness baseline, most of our happiness is grounded in our habitual thoughts, words, and actions.

So happiness is, as they say, an inside job. Happiness is not a destination, not something to be pursued. It is the way we live. There is much wisdom out there to guide us, to inspire us, to encourage us. But, like horses being led to water, we can be led to joy but not made to drink it. Ultimately, it is our choice to live in joy. Or not. That freedom to choose can be both scary (we are responsible and there is no one else to blame) and liberating (we are no longer victims of our circumstances).

Happiness is a choice we make every moment. We can remember happy times in the past, and we can anticipate happy times in the future, but happiness can only be actually experienced in the present moment. So each moment is a new opportunity to choose. If we choose repeatedly to be happy, it becomes a habit, our default position. I think of it as resetting my Internet home page to my happy place. By *happy place*, I don't mean a place of unrelenting inner sunshine. I mean a place of refuge and spiritual sustenance. Of contented fulfillment. Home. A home that, like Dorothy in the *Wizard of Oz*, I never really left. A home that, whether we know it or not, we all live in together. In that sense, our habits become not the way *to* happiness, but rather the way *of* happiness. Then happiness becomes, as Buddha said, simply the way, and the way we live.

Developing joyful habits is the purpose of this book. The title *10 Steps to Finding Your Happy Place (and Staying There)* might sound like there is a way to happiness "out there," and that we can follow the 10 Steps like we would follow the yellow brick road to Oz. But in truth, each of the steps brings us back to where we started, with ourselves. Like finding your glasses on top of your head, you wake up and realize that your happiness was here all along.

A man travels the world over in search of what he needs
and returns home to find it.
—George Moore

Step 1

Give Yourself Permission to Be Happy

Let's start at the very beginning,
A very good place to start.
–"Do Re Mi," The Sound of Music

What are your uncensored thoughts when you think about happiness? Do you feel some resistance? Some anxiety? Fear?

You might be surprised to discover that you are blocking your own happiness with beliefs you are not even aware of. Before we can begin to develop habits to grow a joyful spirit, we need to give ourselves loving and generous permission to be happy.

In this step, we will identify any blocks we have set up, and build a habit of believing that it is truly okay for us to be happy. Not just okay—it is our greatest purpose and our greatest treasure.

Getting Our Happiness Bearings

*Ever since happiness heard your name, it has been
running through the streets trying to find you.*
–HAFIZ

We all want to be happy, but many of us have some secret ambivalence about it. Why would anyone be reluctant to go for the joy gusto? Maybe some of us have reluctance in our genes. My ancestors were Huguenots, Protestants driven out of France to escape slaughter for their religious beliefs. Have you seen any portraits of John Calvin, the theologian these Protestants followed? He does not look like a happy guy.

Maybe you think that happiness is not an appropriate goal when there is so much suffering in the world.

Maybe you think that you shouldn't be happy when people around you are not happy.

Maybe you don't want to tempt fate.

Maybe you are scared to be happy because you are scared you can't make it last.

Maybe it isn't sophisticated in your circle to be happy. (If you are a high school student in a typical urban high school, then for sure it's not cool to be happy.)

Maybe being happy means relaxing your guard, and then all those terrible things you keep at bay by the sheer force of your vigilance will come in the night to destroy you or someone you love.

Do any of these examples resonate for you? If you have discovered some hidden blocks, then that's terrific. Don't judge them. And don't judge yourself for having them! Just be curious. Give yourself credit for bravely taking an honest look. Holding these beliefs in loving awareness will begin to soften them.

Start where you are.
–PEMA CHÖDRÖN

Starter Habits

When my grandson was a newborn, I could spend hours just looking at him. Okay, I still do. I like to look at him, cuddle him, smell him, and just watch him. Watching him sleep is better than watching TV. Who knew that watching someone breathe could be so fascinating?

He is already very wise. For one thing, he knows how to belly breathe. All babies do (which of course makes them all wise). Belly breathing. That means breathing into the lower part of your lungs. This pushes your belly out. We're all born breathing that way. All animals breathe that way.

Somewhere along the way, many of us humans, though, become chest breathers, breathing only into the top part of our lungs. Why do we do that? Maybe because we want to keep our tummies flat. Maybe because of stress. Stress causes us to hold our breath. Holding our breath tells our brains that we are in danger, and that triggers the release of fight-or-flight chemicals, very handy if we are actually being attacked, but usually unnecessary in our day-to-day modern lives. Chronic shallow breathing feeds a loop of stress response, actually creating more stress and releasing more stress chemicals, very damaging over time.

Just as shallow breathing contributes to stress, belly breathing promotes relaxation. It tells our brains that we are safe and releases serotonin and endorphins. Deep breathing pumps more oxygen into our blood, which in turn nourishes our muscles and our brains. I've read that deep breathing can alleviate pain, anxiety, sleep problems, and depression. It helps us remove toxins and improves the immune system. Belly breathing is linked to higher brain function. Higher brain function relates to our attention span, judgment, empathy, learning, forethought, optimism, and self-awareness.

In other words, belly breathing will help us quickly get to and stay in our happy place. I haven't read this anywhere, but I'm hoping it will also help me remember where I left the car keys and why I walked into the kitchen.

I like to think of belly breathing as a starter habit, along with smiling. While belly breathing is telling our brains that we are safe, smiling tells our brains that we are happy. Even a fake smile, through muscle messaging, tells our brains that our glass is half full. Our brain responds with those good feeling chemicals and before we know it, our glass is even more than half full. Smiling also triggers a similar response in others, so we're spreading cheer like Johnny Appleseed.

If all we do is develop these two starter habits, belly breathing and smiling, we will be amazed at how much happier we are.

Smile, breathe, and go slowly.
–THICH NHAT HANH

Fun Is Good!

Many families look forward to the summer: Family vacations. Trips to the beach. Sports. Picnics. Cooking out in the backyard. Enjoying time with the kids.

As a parent, I don't remember it that way. Summers were a stressful time when my son James was a boy. Without the structure of school, his autistic behavior intensified. He had frequent tantrums. He did not like to do what other kids enjoyed, so he did not have friends. He did not like to participate in typical family activities, so family vacations were not something I looked forward to.

I saw summers as opportunities to focus on the autism therapy du jour—auditory training, sensory integration, behavior modification, diet changes, homeopathic treatments, and on and on. With each summer, he grew older and my hope for a cure grew more desperate.

One spring I was talking to James's developmental psychologist. We were going over several options for James's summer. One option I dismissed quickly by saying, "That one would just be fun." The doctor leaned forward until he was sure he had eye contact and I was paying attention. Then he said slowly and deliberately, "Fun ... is ... good."

I guess all those years of training paid off for him, because that was one of the smartest things I ever heard.

> *Laughter is the closest distance between two people.*
> –Victor Borge

Our Greatest Gift

Joy is the most infallible sign of the presence of God.
—Pierre Teilhard de Chardin

We encounter forks in the road every day of our lives. We make choices. Big choices and little choices. Choices that take us in one direction instead of the other. A wide range of factors inform our decisions about which path to choose. Often happiness is not one of those factors. We think about what we should do, or ought to do. We think about a payoff down the road that is appealing to us now. We think about our responsibilities and obligations. We resign ourselves to our fate. A choice based on what will lead to our greatest happiness seems, well, wrong. We might even ask whether living in joy is sort of selfish. That's easy to answer: No. On the contrary, happy people tend to be very generous, whereas unhappy people are often selfish or self-centered. Everything in the universe tells us that happiness is a good thing.

Joy is at the core of all major faith traditions. Great minds are in favor of it. The Bible is full of exhortations to rejoice and be joyful. The Dalai Lama says that happiness is a valid goal — and has observed that the "conscious decision to seek happiness in a systematic manner can profoundly change the rest of our lives." Aristotle said, "Happiness is the meaning and the purpose of life, the whole aim and end of human existence." That might sound glib or even ridiculous, but let's examine it more closely.

The human body tells us it's good to be happy. Happy people are healthier, live longer, and recover more quickly from illness. Happiness strengthens our immune system. We have more energy and stamina. Our brain even works better when we're happy.

Our emotional well-being is supported by happiness. Happy people are more well-adjusted, have higher self-esteem. We are more resilient and rebound faster when faced with life's inevitable challenges and disappointments. Happy people are more creative and productive and successful.

Happiness brings social benefits as well. People like to be around happy people. Our relationships with others are stronger. Our marriages last longer and are more fulfilling. Our friendships are supportive and nurturing. We are better parents. I know this from my own family. At times when things got stressful at home and the kids' moods and behavior deteriorated along with mine, I found that fussing at them was not effective. Neither was yelling or crying or threatening or begging. However, when I would disengage and focus on calming myself and recentering, balance was magically restored and things improved for everyone. Focusing on my own happiness, in appropriate ways of course, helpēd my children find their happy places, too.

Happiness is important to the well-being of individuals and communities and even nations. The Declaration of Independence of the United States protects the pursuit of happiness as an inalienable right. And another country has even made it a government policy. In *The Geography of Bliss,* author Eric Weiner describes how Bhutan, a small kingdom in the Himalayas, focused its resources on nurturing the happiness of its citizens. The government recognized the connection between the country's GDH (gross domestic happiness) and the country's GDP (gross domestic product). Apparently, programs that increase well-being increase the bottom line. I wonder what would happen if, during difficult economic times, we all focused on happiness rather than on government bailouts and military buildups. I'm just sayin'...

I would go so far as to say that being happy is one of the most unselfish and socially responsible things we can do in our lives. An interviewer once asked author and counterculture icon Ken Kesey what he was doing in his later years to make the world a better place. He looked out from his front porch and said, "Well, this year I'm growing asparagus." I'm not famous and no interviewer will ever ask me that question, but if one ever did, I have my answer ready: "This year I'm growing a joyful spirit."

> *Thousands of candles can be lighted from a single candle,*
> *and the life of the candle will not be shortened.*
> *Happiness never decreases by being shared.*
> –UNKNOWN

Wow

When my daughter Mia was young, one of her favorite books was *Lily's Purple Plastic Purse* by Kevin Henkes. I loved this book, too, because the little mouse, Lily, was so much like Mia. They were both feisty fashionistas with an exuberance for life that couldn't be contained and sometimes got them into trouble.

One line repeated throughout Lily's story: "'Wow,'" one of the characters would say, and the narration would add, "That was just about all [that character] could say."

Wow described Mia's attitude about life. I read that *enthusiasm* means "possessed by the gods." That was Mia. Everything was an exciting adventure. Whatever I suggested, Mia was front and center. Did she want to run errands with me? Oh yes indeed, as she headed for the door. Whenever I told her what we were having for dinner, she would shout with glee that it was her favorite food, even if she had never tried it before.

Before I adopted Mia, I had shopped in the same little grocery store for several years without knowing anyone there. But when three-year-old Mia came on the scene, she quickly made friends with everyone who worked there, as well as any number of random shoppers on any given day. While I shopped, she would skip away for a few moments to help Eddie stock the shelves in the dairy section or chat up some shopper in the produce section.

One evening after a busy day at kindergarten, Mia excitedly told me that she had seen the principal putting on lipstick. I thought it was odd that the principal was walking around the school applying makeup. On further inquiry, Mia explained that she had been sent to the principal's office as a consequence of her inability to keep her hands out of classmate Marissa's long hair during storytime. I detected no remorse. On the contrary, seeing the principal putting on her lipstick seemed to Mia like a forbidden and secret wonderfulness that only Mia was honored to observe. The principal and I had a good laugh the next day as we discussed the effectiveness of this consequence for Mia's misbehavior.

Mia coveted Marissa's long hair. Impatient with the slow growth of her own hair, Mia improvised. She took a large pink T-shirt and stretched the neck around her head like a headband so that the T-shirt hung down her back. She became an expert stylist. The T-shirt could be put up in a bun or a ponytail, or (I'm not kidding) braided.

One day as she was heading off to the mall with her grandmother, her T-shirt draping her shoulders like shiny tresses shimmering in a shampoo commercial, she asked me, looking momentarily doubtful, "Will everyone think I have long hair?"

"No," I said, smiling. "Everyone will think you have a pink T-shirt on your head."

She paused, eyeing me suspiciously. Then, with a final flip of the T-shirt, she said confidently, "No, they won't." And off she skipped, laughing and holding her grandmother's hand.

"Wow," I said. That was just about all I could say.

Be happiness itself.
–UNKNOWN

Shadow Beliefs

Once we have convinced ourselves that it's okay to be happy, we might set out to enhance our happiness and deepen our joy. But maybe we seem to make little progress. We feel frustrated and wonder why our efforts don't produce results. Sometimes we hold shadow beliefs that block our happiness. Just as we don't always notice our body's shadow, we might not even be aware of these shadow beliefs. A shadow belief operates at a subliminal level and affects the way we perceive and interact with people and the world around us.

Take me, for example. I was not a very happy person for much of my life. Not that I didn't have happy times. I did. But I did not have a foundation of deep, abiding joy. I had a foundation of anxiety and fear. I believed that I had to stay vigilant. I believed that if I relaxed my guard, terrible things would happen to the people and things I cared about. I was so weighed down by crushing responsibility, much of which I later understood was not even mine.

When I was a little girl, my mother had debilitating headaches and sometimes fainted. Often I was the only one home with her. I would have to get the smelling salts and try to revive her. I was afraid that one day I would not be able to revive her and she would die. Every day I rushed home from school and called for her, terrified that she had died when I was not there to take care of her.

Later, when I became a mother, I felt responsible for my son's autism. My failure to find a cure for him was a personal failure that caused more soul anguish than I have words to describe. In the part of my mind that does not listen to reason, not only was his autism my fault but so was my inability to cure him.

This need to be vigilant permeated so much of my life I didn't even see it. My belief that something horrible would happen if I relaxed my guard was a shadow belief. I didn't understand that I had a choice about my shadow beliefs. I just thought that they were part of how the world worked.

At the root of my fear, anxiety, and heavy sense of responsibility was a belief that I was not safe — in fact, that the world was not safe. I've learned that this is a common shadow belief. Here are some other common ones:

> I'm not good enough.
> I don't deserve love, happiness, success, etc.
> I'm a bad person.
> I can't get over my past.
> People won't like or respect the real me.
> I can't trust my own intuition or judgment.
> Good guys finish last.
> I am powerless.

All of these support the most pervasive shadow belief: It's not okay to be happy.

Einstein said that the most important choice we can make is to decide whether the universe is friendly or hostile. For much of my life, I saw the universe as hostile, full of catastrophes waiting to happen as soon as I relaxed my guard. The eventual realization that this belief was actually a choice, and that I could make a different choice, was a life-changing moment.

So the question is, if we can recognize any of these or other shadow beliefs as a part of us, how do we stop believing in them? Why can't we simply stop thinking this way?

The answer is: Because these shadow beliefs have embedded themselves in our brains as neural pathways, much like wheels create ruts in a dirt road. And just as continuous traffic deepens ruts, so our mental repetition strengthens our thinking habits. Consider for a moment how a fundamental belief in danger everywhere—which was how I saw the world through my shadow belief that I was never safe—affected all the decisions I made, my ability to trust people, my ability to relax and enjoy myself.

This does not have to be permanent. We can replace these shadow beliefs with counter beliefs, simply different beliefs, until the counter beliefs become as habitual as were the shadow beliefs. Counter beliefs interrupt habitual negative thoughts and create positive thinking habits. They create new ruts—this time of joy!

Most people are about as happy
as they make up their minds to be.
–ABRAHAM LINCOLN

Out of the Shadows

I finally saw that much of my worldview was based on beliefs that I could change. That I wanted to change. And after the scary trips to the hospital described in this book's introduction, that I knew I absolutely had to change.

I wanted to make a different choice, but I couldn't just snap my fingers and change my beliefs. I needed to address everything underlying them. I needed to believe that terrible things would not happen if I relaxed my vigilance. Or rather, I needed to believe that terrible things, which do in fact happen sometimes, did not happen *because* I relaxed my vigilance. I needed to give myself permission to be happy.

Joel Osteen, pastor of the largest congregation in the United States, gave a great sermon once about using the delete button to erase negative thoughts and substitute positive ones. Here is how it might work in this context of shadow beliefs and counter beliefs about happiness:

> I don't deserve to be happy. Delete! Joy is my natural state.
> I don't have time to be happy. Delete! There is an eternity
> of joy in every moment.
> It's selfish to be happy. Delete! Joy is my greatest gift to
> the world.

We might start by stating the exact opposite of our shadow belief. For example, if I believe I'm unworthy to be happy, I could choose the counter belief that I am worthy of happiness.

I wrote about my shadow belief that if I relaxed my vigilance, something bad would happen. A counter belief could be: *My happiness does not cause bad things to happen.* Or even simpler—because my shadow belief was based on fear of imagined danger—my counter belief could be: *I am safe.* In fact, this latter one is what I actually told myself every time I felt myself getting anxious and spinning out nightmare what-if scenarios. *I am safe. I am safe. I am safe.* Over time, I truly believed it—and then I lived it!

Sometimes a generic counter belief is helpful enough. For example, no matter our shadow belief and how much detail we know about it, we can say, *Happiness is my greatest purpose.* Or, *It's okay to be happy.* Or, *Fun is good.*

The value of the counter belief is that it interrupts a habitual negative or regressive thought and substitutes a positive or progressive thought, which will become a better, healthier thought habit. Sometimes we might need to play with ideas for counter beliefs until one catches our attention.

We must remember that change is always a process, and our journey toward happiness is no different. First, we become aware of our shadow belief. We catch ourselves when we fall into our habitual shadow thinking. Second, we interrupt our habit by substituting a different thought, what I call a counter belief. Third, we consistently substitute our counter belief every time we catch ourselves in shadow thinking—every single time! Gradually, the counter belief will become the new habitual belief. It will no longer be counter to anything; it will be the standard.

The main thing is not to create stress—no matter our shadow belief, we are always trying to reduce stress! It takes a while to establish a habit. If you are like me, your shadow beliefs have been around for a long time, so be patient and give yourself credit for taking any and all steps to change them. It is worth the effort.

You leave old habits behind by starting out with the thought,
"I release the need for this in my life."
–WAYNE DYER

Pushing the River

Don't push the river. It flows by itself.
—Fritz Perls

My daughter Mia is a natural athlete. She played basketball during her growing up years. She played during the season on her school team and during the off-season in hoop clubs. Then in high school, she wanted to switch to a new sport, lacrosse. But when she came home from the first practice, she announced that she was going to quit. When I asked her why, she said in frustration, "I don't know how to play."

I casually asked her how long she had been playing lacrosse.

She frowned and snorted in exasperation. "Two hours."

"Well," I suggested, "why don't you play two more hours before you decide."

After the second practice, she announced that she loved the game and thought she would be good at it. And she was. She played on the varsity team the last two years of high school. Patience, child.

I have a black belt in tae kwon do. I knew nothing about martial arts when I started and, like everyone does, I started with a white belt. It took me about four years to move through the yellow, green, blue, red, and brown levels to get a black belt. At the beginning, many people progress fairly quickly, but as the skill level gets higher, the minimum length of time between belt promotions gets longer. You can extend the intervals between promotions if you are not ready for the next level, but you can't shorten them. It takes as long as it takes. You learn patience.

Sometimes I am not very patient. Sometimes I lose my way. I wake up somewhere other than my happy place. I feel discouraged and self-critical. I think I should do better and be better and that I should do better and be better *faster*. Sometimes I feel grumpy, and on top of that, I catch myself believing that I *shouldn't* be grumpy. Then I feel worse. Pema Chödrön, an American Buddhist nun, says that this is a subtle aggression against who we really are. Practice "isn't about trying to throw ourselves away and become something better. It's about befriending who we already are."

That is the essence of giving ourselves permission to be happy. Even when we're grumpy. Especially then.

Adopt the pace of nature: her secret is patience.
–Ralph Waldo Emerson

Life Is a Lover

Don't get ahead of your soul. The goal isn't to get somewhere. The goal isn't about forcing something to happen. The goal is to be in harmony with the gifts that are already given. The goal is to fall in love with your life.
–Paula D'Arcy

In a recent sermon, my minister told the story of a friend's funeral. The eulogy included the observation, "For him, life was not a dark mystery to be anxious about. For him, life was a lover."

What a concept: life as a lover. What if we greeted life as we would greet a lover—with passion, eagerness, anticipation, joy, pleasure? How would our lives change if we thought about life this way?

For so many years, I treated life as an adversary, not as a lover, and as an adversary that usually won the round. Things didn't work out the way I wanted. My baby had autism. My relationships ended. Tired—no, exhausted with my life as it was, I finally realized that the common denominator in all my disappointments was…me. I set out to change myself.

I had a friend named Faye, a Mississippi steel magnolia. She was five feet tall on a good day and couldn't have weighed more than ninety-five pounds soaking wet. No matter how casual the occasion, she wore spike heels and carried herself like a runway model. She was as feisty as a bantam rooster. One day when she was being her hilarious self, I said, "Faye, you are too much." She drew herself up and puffed out her chest and said in her sweetest Southern drawl, "Oh no, honey, I am just right."

And she was. More than just right. Ridiculously extraordinary. As are we all. These days I would be more likely to describe life as a friend than as an adversary. A good friend. And I have a new vision of possibility—life as a lover. Now where are my dancing shoes? Never mind, I'll dance barefoot.

> *I have found that if you love life, life will love you back.*
> —Artur Rubinstein

Dropping Our Stories

I give presentations on happiness, so the following story really resonates with me. And, of course, it's not just about public speaking.

A speaker was trying to contact the man in charge of a retreat for which she had been hired. She called and asked for him. The person who answered the phone said he wasn't there. The speaker left a message for him to call her back. He didn't call so, the next day, she called again. The person who answered said he wasn't there. Again, the speaker left a message. And again, the retreat facilitator didn't call her back. On the third day, the speaker called once more. The person who answered the phone politely told her that the man she was trying to reach wasn't there. At this point, feeling frustrated, the speaker blurted out in exasperation, "Well, maybe this means that I shouldn't be speaking at your retreat." The other person paused and then said thoughtfully, "Maybe it just means he isn't here right now."

Ah, the stories we tell ourselves.

I was in therapy for several years. About a year after I finished, I was reflecting on how good my life was, and I attributed that in no small part to my therapist. I thought it would be nice to let her know how much I appreciated her contribution to my well-being. I called and left her a voice message asking if I could stop by, explaining a little of the reason. She did not return my call.

A few months after that, I happened to run into her. She apologized for not calling and said she would soon. She didn't. At this point, I felt confused and a bit angry. I knew her to be a conscientious, highly ethical professional, so this lapse seemed out of character. I wondered if I had done something to offend her. I kept thinking about our last communications, looking for something I had said that she might have taken the wrong way.

The not knowing was so uncomfortable that I was willing to make up all kinds of stories. My favorite one was that this was some sort of therapy final exam. That is, if I could cope with being rejected by my therapist, then I must be very well adjusted indeed! A Woody Allen sort of explanation. As ridiculous as it was, that one brought me some degree of comfort. Still, it didn't stop my wondering.

I finally wrote the therapist a letter, telling her what I had wanted to say face to face. I thanked her for her expertise and patience. I expressed my gratitude for what she had meant to me in my life, recognizing that my present and future joy were considerably enhanced by what I had learned under her guidance. I wished her well and said good-bye.

I was somewhat surprised that she responded immediately and graciously. She explained that she had been dealing with some personal issues and had become distracted, and she sincerely apologized for her unprofessional behavior. It had nothing to do with me. I told her some of the things I had imagined as the reasons for her ignoring me. We had a good laugh about some of them.

We choose the stories we tell ourselves. Even better, we can choose not to tell ourselves any stories at all and just pay attention to what is really happening.

I could choose to see this differently.
—A Course in Miracles

Reality Check

In the book *You Are Not Your Brain*, the stories we tell ourselves are called deceptive brain messages. Our brains tell us thousands of these messages every day. I've read that we think forty thousand to sixty thousand thoughts a day. Of these, 80 percent are habitual thoughts, and most of those habitual thoughts are negative. That's a lot of habitual negative thinking.

But how do we know which messages are deceptive? I have discovered two questions that help me. If I am spinning out one of my negative stories about something that has happened, I ask myself, *Do I know for a fact that this is true?* For example, I spun stories of all the things I might have done to offend my former therapist. I could have stopped that runaway train of thoughts by asking if I knew for sure that any of those stories were true. The answer would have been no.

If I need reinforcement to counter the deceptive brain messages, I ask myself, *Is it possible that there is a different explanation?* The answer is usually yes. For example, in that scenario, I might have asked myself, *Is it possible that something that doesn't have anything to do with me kept the therapist from responding?* The answer would have been yes.

Once I realize that I don't know for sure that my negative story is true and that there is possibly—even probably—a different explanation for what has happened, the negative story loop replaying in my head is interrupted and it is easier to let go of my drama.

My daughter Grace tends to move through the world as the star in her own soap opera. She feels buffeted by the winds of fate as she careens from one crisis to another. One day we sat down and I reflected back to her the storyline she was telling herself. She saw that she was the screenwriter and therefore had the ability to write something different. On one side of an index card we wrote, *I am creating this drama.* On the other side, we used a line from *A Course in Miracles*: *I could choose to see this differently.* She still carries the card with her, and when she senses her anger or anxiety ramping up, she pulls it out and reads it to herself until she can disengage from the self-made tall tale.

Some of us might be thinking, *Okay, but it is also possible that our negative story is true.* That's right, but we usually don't immediately know that for sure. We might find out only in the fullness of time that our negative story is true, but we can deal with it then. We also might never know. Either way, we can choose to drop the currently unverified story that is blocking our happiness and peace of mind in the present moment. Because if a negative story turns out to be false, like mine usually do, we can save ourselves a lot of needless worry.

> *Nothing real can be threatened. Nothing unreal exists.*
> *Herein lies the peace of God.*
> —*A COURSE IN MIRACLES*

Powerful Beyond Measure

Our deepest fear is not that we are inadequate. Our deepest
fear is that we are powerful beyond measure. It is our light,
not our darkness that most frightens us.
—A COURSE IN MIRACLES

Why are we afraid of our own power? Why is unworthiness such a common shadow belief? My mother struggled with feelings of unworthiness all her life. Even in her final months, this was the theme of her conversations with her pastor. No matter how much she had accomplished in her life, no matter how many people's lives were better because of her, no matter what assurances she got from her friends, her family, and her pastor, they were not enough to make her believe that she was worthy of love and happiness.

And I inherited her belief, as perhaps she had inherited it from her mother. Eventually there came a moment when I felt overcome with shame, shame that I couldn't identify. I didn't know why I felt it. I couldn't connect it to any specific memory or event. It was like the dementors from the Harry Potter stories had found me and were sucking the life force, the very soul, from my being. The shame was terrifying and suffocating. I thought I would die from it. And at the moment when I thought I could not stand it another second, when I was about literally to bolt from the room and run screaming into the street, I heard a voice, soft and gentle and loving. The voice whispered in my spirit, *It is not yours.*

Like awaking from a nightmare in a cold sweat, I looked around, a bit disoriented. Who said that? What wasn't mine? The elephant got up off my chest and left the room, which suddenly filled with golden light. It was like an infected cyst of unworthiness had been surgically removed. The shame disappeared like fog burned up by the sun. It wasn't mine. I let it go. And walked out into a new world.

> *Well, if you want to sing out*
> *Sing out.*
> *And if you want to be free*
> *Be free.*
> *'Cause there's a million things to be.*
> *You know that there are.*
> –CAT STEVENS

The Person of Yes

A certain political party, it doesn't matter which one (this isn't a political commentary), is sometimes called the party of no. I get that. I often catch myself being the person of no.

"Hey, do you want to come with us to...?" No.
"Mom, is it all right if I...?" No.
"We need someone to..." No.
"Wouldn't it be a great idea to...?" No.
"What if I tried to...?" No.

I don't want to be the person of no. I want to be the person of yes. A person of yes doesn't always actually say yes—a person of yes uses what she has and steps up when needed. And sometimes does say yes, just because it's fun!

One Sunday morning, a guest preacher was scheduled to speak in my church. The worship service started, and there was no sign of the guest preacher. It was time for the sermon, and there was no guest preacher. There was the title of the guest speaker's sermon, which had been typed in the bulletin: "Using What You've Got." One of the associate pastors looked around nervously and stood up. He used what he had: a title and some willingness. It was a terrific sermon. I wish I remembered all the words he said. I do remember watching him and thinking, *This is what faith looks like.* The pastor didn't talk about faith. He showed us faith. He used what he had and said yes.

My two autistic sons live in a group home for adults. The home is run by a remarkable organization, Edwards Center. Staff people help them with various things: cooking, money, transportation. One staff person in particular goes above and beyond. When she took James to the zoo, one of his favorite places, she made it a creative outing. She videotaped him talking about the animals. James lectured, sang, and danced his way through the zoo. I got the DVD for Mother's Day. It was like a show on Animal Planet. I treasure it because it is James at his best—happy, being a ham, showing off what he knows about what he loves. The staff person made this possible. She used what she had and said yes.

Come to think of it, so did James.

For all that has been, thanks. For all that will be...yes.

–DAG HAMMARSKJÖLD

Show Me the Miracles!

I wake today with miracles correcting
my perception of all things. And so begins the day.
−A COURSE IN MIRACLES

Did you ever see the movie *Jerry McGuire*? Tom Cruise plays a sports agent trying to stay in business. His only client is a football player played by Cuba Gooding Jr. In a famous scene, Gooding repeatedly yells at Cruise, "Show me the money!"

In her book *Glad No Matter What*, SARK (pen name for Susan Ariel Rainbow Kennedy) suggests going on miracle walks. Just go for a walk with no particular destination. Like the character in the movie, look around and say to the universe, "Show me the miracles!" And then practice recognizing them. This might take some vision adjustment. Look around. See the grass pushing through the concrete sidewalk? What about the person who returns your smile? Do you hear the birds chirping? Don't forget that you are walking, that you can see, that you can hear.

This idea isn't limited to walks. You can look for miracles at any time in any place. Maybe an old friend will call you out of the blue and reconnect. Maybe you will find a lucky penny. Maybe even in the midst of something that seems challenging or sad, you can find a miracle. What if you can't walk or see or hear? You are alive, and that is an amazing miracle right there. Our hearts beat, our lungs breathe, our brains think.

I woke up today with miracles on my mind. And in my heart. I don't know what this day will bring, but I know it will be good. It started with a quick trip to the dentist to file a rough spot off my tooth that my OCD tongue wouldn't leave alone. In an instant, my tooth was smooth. A miracle!

I came home and picked blueberries and raspberries in the garden to put on my cereal. I ate my cereal on the patio as I watched that naughty squirrel on the bird feeder. I have moved the feeder away from all the bushes, I have put a squirrel guard on the post, and still I find him nestled in sunflower seeds. I don't know how he gets up there. A miracle! At least to him.

The day seems full of promise and possibility. I don't wake up every day feeling this way, but I did today. A miracle for sure.

I took my son James to see the Broadway musical *The Lion King*. We had seats on the main floor on the aisle not far from the stage. When the music started, the animals marched in through side doors and down the aisle to the stage. If you have seen the show or any ads or news about the show, you know that the costuming is magical and the actors are channeling the animal spirits.

The animals paraded right by us. When the elephant lumbered by, James turned to me with eyes so wide and a smile brighter than the stage lights and whispered, "Is that a real elephant?" A miracle. I wept with delight.

We can find miracles even in our darkest moments. A blogger I admire writes about her son who has leukemia. She calls him Superman Sammy. She describes the day they got the diagnosis as their "lucky day." She explains that they were at the doctor for a different reason altogether and discovered the leukemia almost by accident. Still hard to see the lucky part, but here it is: If they had not discovered the leukemia that day and started treatment immediately, Sammy would not be here today to wow the world with his wonderfulness. When I read her description of the diagnosis day as a lucky day, all I could think was, *That is a mom with some serious miracle mojo.*

Albert Einstein said, "There are only two ways to live your life. You can live as if nothing is a miracle, or you can live as if everything is a miracle."

Well, when you put it that way...

> *Look with your eyes and hear with your ears, and pay attention to everything I am going to show you, for that is why you have been brought here.*
> —EZEKIEL 40:4

The Power to Choose

*The most common way people give up their power
is by thinking they don't have any.*
–ALICE WALKER

There was a series of Capital One credit card commercials that
featured villainous Vikings, representing exorbitant fees and other
scary credit company practices, charging toward hapless shopping
victims. At the last moment, however, someone would divert the im-
minent horribleness by whipping a Capital One credit card out of
a purse or wallet. The menacing Vikings would stop in their tracks
and retreat in disappointment. The commercials always ended with
the question, "What's in *your* wallet?"

I got to wondering what's in my wallet. My spiritual wallet, that is.
What do I carry with me to ward off soul-marauding Vikings?

When I was young and knew everything, I wrote a philosophy
paper based on the premise that we participate in creating the reality
we perceive. In the arrogance of youth, I thought I came up with that
idea myself. Well, of course I didn't think of it first, or last, and better
minds than mine have explained it more fully. But somehow I knew
that I had untapped potential to shape my world.

Sadly, the world I shaped for most of my life was not a kind one.
To paraphrase Montaigne, it was a world of terrible misfortunes,

most of which never happened. Like the lookout in a Western, I kept watch by the fire during the night, always on alert, always vigilant. And when some bad things inevitably did happen, I believed it was because my guard had dropped, because I had closed my eyes for a moment for some much-needed rest.

Even as I write the words, I shake my head in disbelief that I lived that way for so long. If necessity is the mother of invention, then exhaustion is the mother of major life changes.

A Course in Miracles teaches that there is another way of looking at the world. A way of peace, a way of compassion, a way of happiness, a way of connection, a way of loving awareness. In the words of the *Tao Te Ching*, "the eternal way."

I live in a different universe now, a friendly one. I can't prove that it is friendly. I simply choose to believe that it is. And that choice drives my perceptions and experiences. Does that mean that I close my eyes to the suffering in the world? Do I ignore tragedies like 9/11 and natural disasters? No. But if my worldview is shaped by love rather than by fear, then these events trigger compassion and reaching out rather than anger or defensiveness and retreating inside.

So what's in my spiritual wallet? A credit card of power with no limit. Not power over my circumstances but power over how I interpret them and interact with them. The power of choice.

And guess what. That's what's in your wallet, too.

> *I believe that the very purpose of our life is to seek happiness.*
> —THE DALAI LAMA

Step 2

Decide if You Want to Be Right or Happy

Don't fight a battle if you won't gain anything by winning.
–General George S. Patton

As we go through our daily lives, many times we are offered a choice to insist on our "rightness" or to let it go. Many of us choose to prove our point, to get in the last word, to enlighten the benighted souls who dare to disagree. But even if we "win," our enjoyment of victory is often short-lived, and we are left feeling vaguely unsettled or dissatisfied.

In this step, we will take a look at that need to prevail at all costs. We might find out that the person who pays the highest cost for our rightness is us. And while there could be situations that call for us to hold our ground, we can develop a habit of discerning when to hold firm and when to yield. We can, in other words, learn to pick our battles.

I'm Right—So What!

My daughter stormed into the house after school. She had had an argument with a friend. As she described the argument, she became more and more puffed up with her own sense of rightness. She grew angrier and angrier with her friend's stubborn, bull-headed refusal to see what was the incontrovertible, inescapable, clear-as-the-nose-on-your-face-you-must-be-a-moron-not-to-see-it rightness of my daughter's position.

I listened without comment. When she finally began to wind down and looked to me for validation of her outrage, I simply said with a smile, "Who cares?" Well, that was not what she was expecting. While she was standing there with her mouth agape, momentarily speechless, I jumped in before she could protest. "Do you want to be right or to be happy?" I asked. I asked her to think about the topic of their argument and to consider whether being right about that topic was worth the emotional upset she was experiencing. As she did a quick cost-benefit analysis, I could see her body relax and her spirit calm.

Once, I was having lunch in a restaurant with some colleagues. I ordered something that had a French name. As soon as I said it, the server corrected my pronunciation. I speak French passably well and lived in French-speaking countries for several years, so I was confident that I had pronounced the dish correctly. In turn,

I corrected the server, with a not-so-subtle I-know-better-than-you tone. After he left the table, I commented on how rude he was. Even if he had been right, what bad form to correct someone in front of other people. The nerve! (I can hear you laughing. Can we say, pot calling the kettle black?) I went on and on about it, and by the time my food came, I was too agitated to enjoy it.

As I'm writing this, I am thinking back to several times when I committed a faux pas (yes, I appreciate the irony of using a French term here) in front of someone who was in a position to cause me great embarrassment by pointing it out. In each instance, the person said nothing. In one instance, the person even went further by quietly correcting the mistake I made so that no one else would notice what I had done. Much later, when I realized my mistakes, I was so humbled by the graciousness of those people. My mistakes, in the big scheme of life, were minor, but the kindness of their actions was immense.

> *Yield and overcome*
> *Bend and be straight*
> *Empty and be full*
> *Wear out and be new*
> *Have little and gain*
> *Have much and be confused*
> –TAO TE CHING

One Hand Clapping

Being right is not all it's cracked up to be. Think about all the things people argue about. Make a quick list of five things. Let's see—here are the first five things I thought of:

1. Whether we should have a single-payer health-care system
2. Whether a certain misbehaving NFL quarterback should be suspended
3. Whether any particular religion is the only way to God
4. Who really discovered America
5. Whether the toilet paper should roll over the top or from underneath

Ann Landers devoted a number of columns to that last one. No kidding.

Many questions that people spend a lot of time arguing about don't have an objectively discernible right answer. Take the God question, for example. How can people be so sure that their way is the only way? My mom said once with great conviction that something was against the moral laws of the universe. *Wow,* I thought, *how does Mom know what the moral laws of the entire universe are?*

Sometimes even when there is a right answer, it doesn't stop the argument. For example, the Nazis really did kill millions of people. And Obama really was born in Hawaii. But the arguments continue.

Even though I'm a lawyer and trained to argue, winning an argument doesn't always make me happy. Being right must be its own reward, because often there isn't much else to gain from it. At some point I decided that in many instances, being happy was more important to me than being right. Tough on my ego, but nourishing to my spirit.

When poised to do battle, I try to ask myself first if the issue even has a right answer. If it doesn't, then there may be no reason to fight. If there is a right answer, does it matter? For example, I was at a business meeting not long ago. Someone was wondering about something that happens to be my area of expertise. When I offered the correct information, the speaker disagreed with me. I pressed. He pushed back. My ego knickers were in a knot. I was poised to pull out my expert status and crush all opposition, but I paused. The resolution of the issue was not relevant to the meeting topic.

I let it go. My ego sulked. My spirit smiled.

Do I put this into practice at every opportunity? I wish. But when I do, there is a positive shift in my world, a reminder that letting go of being right is often a small sacrifice for living in joy.

> *The world is divided into people who think they are right.*
> –TARA BRACH

I would prefer a world undivided by people who choose to be happy.

Beyond Right and Wrong

*Out beyond the ideas of wrongdoing and right doing,
there is a field. I'll meet you there.*
—Rumi

We are so conditioned to think about issues in terms of right and wrong. This can lead to unnecessary anxiety. My daughter Grace is always the last one to order in a restaurant. She is simply paralyzed by the fear of making the wrong choice. Instead of thinking that there might be several right choices—that is, choices that she would enjoy—she is convinced that there is one, and only one, choice that will make her meal a pleasant experience.

For some reason, we are uncomfortable with the possibility of multiple right answers. In an article in *O, the Oprah Magazine,* Martha Beck called this being "on the horns of a dual-emma." It makes our little synapses sizzle and short out. Our world becomes more fluid. We lose our sense of security. It can be terrifying.

What is it about being right that is so compelling? Is it fear? Is it ego? Is it greed? How can we stop ourselves before we get locked into a way of thinking that permits only one right answer? That permits only one person to be right?

When I think back to some times when it seemed most imperative for me to be right, I can, with the benefit of hindsight, see fear. The fear was usually hidden behind anger and self-righteousness. My aggressive assertion of my rightness in those situations was a need to control what felt out of control. I mistakenly believed that what was out of control was "out there," usually in the form of another person. But I came to understand, with compassion, that what was out of control was me.

When I now feel that urge to engage in battle, I try to pause and look more deeply within. It makes me squirm. I feel so powerful when I am thundering with righteous indignation. I feel so vulnerable when I shine light on the scared places within.

I've learned from Buddhist monk Thich Nhat Hanh's teachings to cradle my feelings, especially the feelings that make me uncomfortable. If I can sit with my discomfort, breathe into it (breathe at all, for that matter!), I feel the discomfort soften. My body relaxes. My mind clears. I can see the gray areas. I can see the middle way, beyond right and wrong.

Be quick to hear, slow to speak, slow to anger.
    −JAMES 1:19.

A Problem Solver's Problem

I'm a problem solver. For most of my life, I have viewed this as one of my greatest strengths. And it is. Except when it isn't.

If my problem is that I'm out of clean socks, then I can solve it by doing the laundry. But if my problem is that my son is autistic, then, try as I might, and try as I did for years, I cannot solve it. Years of various therapies improved my son James's life, but they did not cure what I saw as the problem of his autism.

The problem with my problem-solving approach in that situation is that I saw his autism as a problem, a problem with one solution—which was to make him not autistic. When I couldn't solve the problem, I saw myself as a failure. I had a son who was not "okay," and I wasn't okay, either.

I've come to understand that there are limits to problem solving as an approach to every challenge. As Pema Chödrön says, "Problem solving is based first on thinking there is a problem and second on thinking there is a solution. The concepts of problem and solution can keep us stuck in thinking that there is…a right way and a wrong way." She suggests a different approach, one that focuses on "working *with* rather than struggling *against*."

My epiphany regarding this approach came from none other than James himself, who has never seen his autism as a problem. He has never seen himself as not okay.

Eschewing a right/wrong problem-solving approach to challenges requires a relinquishment of control, a willingness to keep an open mind, a tolerance for not knowing what will happen. And sometimes a humbling of the ego.

I'm still a problem solver. But I've learned that my problem-solving skills are useful in some situations and not in others. I'm still learning to tell the difference.

Enlightenment is the ego's ultimate disappointment.

– CHÖGYAM TRUNGPA RINPOCHE

Nice Idea, But...

Our ancient habitual patterns will start to soften,
and we'll begin to see the faces and hear the words
of people who are talking to us.
–Pema Chödrön

As someone observed in a comment on my blog about choosing to be happy instead of asserting one's rightness, "Wonderful to consider and complex to live."

But we want to live it. So how can we live it, despite, or in harmony with, its complexity? How can we stop ourselves before we get hooked in an argument that creates a chasm between us and our fellow humans rather than a bridge? What techniques or reminders can we use to soften those ancient habitual patterns of seeing everything and everyone in terms of right and wrong?

This seems especially relevant in today's climate of entrenched political stalemates, religious zealotry, and all sorts of us/them fanaticism. When we care deeply about something, or when we are feeling threatened, our ability even to see, much less respect, any other view is limited. For example, as I write this, 2012 is shaping up to be an election year in the United States that already has me feeling edgy.

So I'm trying to remember 2008. I had a lot of opinions about the presidential election that year, opinions I felt very strongly about.

I was blessed to have a friend whose opinions did not match mine. I say blessed because so many other people around me shared my views. I could voice an observation confident that it would be received with nodding heads and murmured support. I was in a virtual gated community of homogeneous worldviews. Except for this one friend.

Throughout the primaries and campaigns, we debated. I was challenged to step out of my comfort zone and listen, really listen. I became aware of the language I used, careful to distinguish fact from interpretation, mindful of the difference between reasoned judgment and personal attack. I had to acknowledge that both of us cared very much about our country *and* (not *but*) had very different views about what our country needed.

The months of debate did not change our respective votes, but I was changed. I learned that when faced with someone who did not agree with me, I could be curious instead of critical. I could listen instead of lecture. I could respect rather than reject. And most important, I could connect rather than separate.

Blessed are the peacemakers.
—MATTHEW 5:9

The Curiosity of Not Knowing

I saw a beautiful photo on a blog. There was a row of curved shapes that caught the eye and sparked the imagination. The photographer invited readers to guess what it was. I couldn't. My mind tried out all sorts of ideas, but nothing clicked into place. I felt uneasy and even a bit insecure, thinking everyone but me would be able to identify it. Even after she told her readers what it was, a park bench, I still couldn't "see" it, and that made me even more agitated.

Most of us have had the experience of misidentifying even something that we can see or hear. For example, one time I heard a noise in the distance that I immediately classified as a train, but a few seconds later I heard more clearly that it was a dog barking. How on earth did my mind register train when a barking dog doesn't sound anything like a train? There is the story of the man who sat up all night terrified of the snake sleeping in the corner, only to see with the dawn's light that it was a coiled rope. At least a rope is more like a snake than a dog barking is like a train roaring closer.

We've all heard that nature abhors a vacuum. Our minds, I think, abhor uncertainty. Our minds are not comfortable just resting in not knowing. Any answer seems better than no answer. Our minds would rather grasp quickly at a wild guess, and then correct the perception when more information becomes available. We are more afraid of uncertainty than we are of physical pain. I wonder why that is. Why is pausing in uncertainty so terrifying that we would rather be moaning on the floor in agony, or ridiculously wrong? What happens in that nanosecond between the stimulus and the attachment of a label? It must seem a dark and scary place for our brains to want to move through it so quickly.

In mindfulness training, that nanosecond is called the gap. In *A Course in Miracles*, it's called "the holy instant." Within that tiny space is an entire universe of possibility, an eternity of wonder. The price of admission? Tolerating the groundlessness of uncertainty.

How do we do that? In her book *Comfortable with Uncertainty*, Pema Chödrön suggests becoming curious, curious about whatever our experience is. Maybe we feel confused, angry, afraid, happy, excited, bored. Before we start putting labels on our experience, before we start judging it, before we start telling ourselves stories about it, we can pause, perhaps just long enough to take a breath, and pay attention with open interest and curiosity.

Everything is interesting if we pause and look with an open mind.

Sometime, somewhere you take something to be the truth. But if you cling to it too strongly, then even when the truth comes in person and knocks on your door, you will not open it.
　　　　　　　　　　　　　　　—UNKNOWN

No One Wins in Court

The first thing we do, let's kill all the lawyers.
—Shakespeare

As someone who spent her career as a lawyer, I've heard all the lawyer jokes. Some are actually funny. The one from Shakespeare is often used out of context. In fact, the speaker was a follower of an anarchist seeking to overthrow the government and install himself as king. The speaker was not criticizing lawyers. On the contrary, he was observing that any tyrant wannabe would have to eliminate the front-line defenders of order and justice—that is, the lawyers—before proceeding with his evil plans. While there are lawyers who undeniably give the profession a bad name, in my career I found most lawyers to be exactly what they should be: healers. That's right. Healers. Someone said once that there are three healing professions: medicine heals the body, ministry heals the soul, and law heals society.

One of the classes I taught was a seminar on drafting contracts. Students come into law school full of a lifetime of TV shows about lawyers in court. They think in terms of drafting a contract that will "hold up" in court. Imagine their surprise when I tell them that if their contract ever ends up in court, they've already lost. A successful contract is not one that "wins" in court. It's one that succeeds before needing a judge and jury; it promotes a good relationship between the parties, encouraging them to perform willingly, and providing something they value in return. If the parties end up in court, our adversarial system results in a winner and a loser, and both parties have lost the relationship they initially envisioned, not to mention the practical losses in time and money.

The United States is known, justifiably so, as a litigious society. We look to the courts to settle all sorts of disputes, from presidential elections to environmental cleanups to neighbors fighting over fences. All these lawsuits have one thing in common: other modes of resolution have failed. And while it may be true that, more often than not, justice is served by the outcome in court, something perhaps more precious is always lost. An adversarial dispute costs us the opportunity we have as individuals, organizations, companies, and governments to find a way to maintain our connection with each other, to have an open hand rather than an upper hand, to find common ground rather than legally superior ground.

Justice is sometimes a sad victor.

> *Therefore when the Tao is lost, there is goodness.*
> *When goodness is lost, there is kindness.*
> *When kindness is lost, there is justice.*
> *When justice is lost, there is ritual.*
> *Now ritual is the husk of faith and loyalty,*
> *the beginning of confusion.*
> –TAO TE CHING

The Way of No Way

If you meet the Buddha, kill the Buddha.
—LIN-CHI

That opening quote is a bit startling, isn't it? Disrespectful, to say the least. What could it mean?

As I understand it, the point of this get-your-attention statement is that we should not be imprisoned by our preconceptions or traditions. In the language of the Bible, we should not bow down before idols, any idol. The idol is not God. It is an illusion.

When I was younger, I spent some time as a back-to-the-land hippie. I believed that civilization was irredeemably corrupt and should be abandoned altogether in favor of a simpler, rural life in harmony with nature. Not just for me, but for you, too. How I disdained the unenlightened urban clods watching TV in their air-conditioned living rooms, eating processed food that was made of who-knew-what, sucking up precious electric and natural-resources energy like junkies. What I remember more than anything is how sure I was that I was right. That I had *the* answer. I was an insufferable boor as I looked down my nose and tried to explain to my family and friends the superior virtues of my view, the only view that mattered. Of course, now I am writing this on my computer in my comfortable city home. And I might have some powdered-sugar doughnuts for a snack later while I'm watching *The Closer*.

We can do the same thing with faith. We can be so sure that our belief is the only right belief. This kind of thinking is an illusion, an idol, and it led to the Crusades and to 9/11. We can believe so strongly in a God of love that we are willing to kill those who disagree. The unbelievers. Those not like us. Or if not kill, then to condemn them to everlasting hell.

Chögyam Trungpa Rinpoche used the term *spiritual materialism* to describe those of us who idolize our creeds as much as we do our cars and computers. Who use our faith to fluff up our egos, to compare ourselves to those less fortunate who do not share our spiritual superiority.

Bruce Lee understood this concept. He revolutionized martial arts with a controversial new approach that he described as "the way of no way." Instead of the set moves and rigid techniques of a particular style, the idea was to use any and all forms of combat as appropriate. No way as way. No limitation as limitation. Awareness unfettered by dogma. He killed the Buddha.

> *The Tao that can be told is not the eternal Tao. The name that can be named is not the eternal name.*
> —TAO TE CHING

No Right Way

When Zen master Katagiri-roshi was sick with terminal cancer, his students watched him closely, nervous about seeing their teacher so frail, so...human. One day he gathered his students around his bed and said, "You want to see how a Zen master dies. I'll show you." The students held their breath and waited for something profound, perhaps magical. Suddenly he kicked and flailed frantically, shouting, "I don't want to die! I don't want to die!" They jumped back. Then he stopped and spoke quietly. "I don't know how I will die. There is no right way."

I spent a lot of my earlier life trying to do it right. Trying to present myself in a certain way, terrified that someone would see the real me. And who was that? I didn't even know. It was exhausting. Thank goodness I'm older now. Not necessarily any wiser, but definitely too tired to care. If my daughter is horrified by what I'm wearing to the store, then too bad. If my students ask me a question I don't know the answer to, then great! We'll find the answer together and all learn something new.

After I got my black belt in tae kwon do, I started learning how to use nunchaku. More commonly known as nunchucks, these martial arts weapons are made of two short sticks connected by a chain. Because the moves are made by swinging the nunchucks with speed, it's hard to learn the moves in slow motion. Or with precision, at least at the beginning. I asked a lot of questions about exactly where my feet should be or the correct angle for certain moves. Like chewing gum and walking at the same time, I was having problems coordinating all the parts of my body. The instructor finally said that there was no one right way. I should just keep practicing to become more comfortable with the weapon and find my own way of doing it. Oh yes, and have fun, he added over my grunts of frustration.

Like the Zen master's students, I was searching for the one right way when all along the way was there before me — because it was my way, whatever that was. I would never move exactly like my teacher. And that was okay.

I once sat next to the former choir director in church. She has a lovely voice. I don't. I was momentarily intimidated when singing hymns. Then I thought, what the heck, and started making a joyful noise to the Lord.

That's how I want to live my life now. I want to make a joyful noise. In my own way.

Sometimes it is better to be kind than to be right. We do not need an intelligent mind that speaks, but a patient heart that listens.
— UNKNOWN

Be Water

In a controversy, the instant we feel anger we have already ceased striving for the truth and have begun striving for ourselves.
—Unknown

I particularly remember one of my former tai chi instructor's exercises. He would stand face-to-face with a student, about half an arm's length apart. Feet were stationary and should not move. The student would push the teacher, trying to force the teacher to take a step back to maintain his balance. As the student pushed on his shoulders or chest, the teacher simply melted away from the touch without avoiding it or resisting it. It was like trying to push water.

At some point, the student would be so extended that the teacher, using only his thumb and forefinger, would lightly grasp the student's wrist and with a small, subtle move throw the student to the ground. No matter how many times we participated in this exercise and vowed not to be caught off balance, our efforts to push invariably resulted in a quick trip to the floor while the teacher remained serenely unaffected and unmoved.

I have learned over the years that many arguments can be handled the same way. The best way to win an argument is to make the issue a nonissue. If there is nothing to fight about, the argument disappears.

There used to be a lot of fighting about money in our house. The kids would want something that I said no to. Or the kids would argue about some perceived inequality. "You bought her new jeans, so you have to buy me new jeans," one would say about another even though I had just bought her new shoes. Or someone would not be satisfied with a less expensive version of the desired designer goods.

Then an amazingly brilliant friend shared the money method in her family, which I quickly adapted for mine. On the first of each month, I gave each child the same amount of money. I continued to pay for food, shelter, and education, but the kids had to pay for everything else with their own money. That included all their clothes, entertainment, birthday presents for friends, etc. When the money was gone, then that was it for the month. No credit and no borrowing from anybody else.

Everyone was treated the same and had control over his or her financial priorities. I retained veto power over purchases, of course, but I exercised it mainly when there was concern for safety or decency. The fighting stopped immediately, because there was nothing to fight about. The bonus was that the kids learned to budget, save, and be careful and thoughtful shoppers. It was undoubtedly one of the best things I ever did as a parent.

The point here is that, thanks to my friend's idea, I was able to make money a nonissue. Now when I find myself in conflict, I try to pause and explore the possibility of reframing the issue to avoid opposing sides. I have found this to be a powerful as well as a peaceful approach.

Empty your mind, be formless, shapeless—like water. Now you put water into a cup, it becomes the cup, you put water into a bottle, it becomes the bottle, you put it in a teapot, it becomes the teapot. Be water, my friend.
—BRUCE LEE

What I Know for Sure

A university professor went to visit a famous Zen master. While the master quietly served tea, the professor talked on and on and on about what he knew of Zen. The master poured the visitor's cup to the brim, and then kept pouring. The professor watched the overflowing cup until he could no longer restrain himself. "It's overflowing! No more will go in!" the professor blurted. "You are like this cup," the master replied. "How can I show you Zen unless you first empty your cup?"

My mind feels like that cup sometimes. So full. Overflowing full. I have a hard time remembering things. My daughter says I have the memory of a gnat. She's right. I think it's because I have so much useless stuff stuck in my memory, and I can't find the delete button. I can remember my childhood phone number, but I can't remember to pick up juice on the way home. When I try to remember something new, my mind plays a familiar recording: *The message inbox for the number you are calling is full.*

There is just too much information from out there that I'm trying to store in here. Not only grocery lists, but also opinions about truth. I just finished a book by someone who thinks he has God all figured out. The title of this particular book isn't important because there are a million books like that. There are a million books like that because there are a million people who believe they know the truth.

Oprah Winfrey writes a column for her magazine every month called "What I Know for Sure." Whenever I pick up her magazine in the checkout line and flip to the back page where this column appears, I marvel at the notion that once a month, like clockwork, she knows something for sure. No wonder she "makes bank," as my daughter says.

So if these people really know the truth, then why don't they all agree?

The *Tao Te Ching* teaches, "Wise men don't need to prove their point. Men who need to prove their point aren't wise." I must be very wise, because not only do I not need to prove my point but I'm not sure I even have a point to prove.

> *You can't organize truth. That's like trying to put*
> *a pound of water into wrapping paper and shaping it.*
> —BRUCE LEE

Silence Is Golden

Those who know do not talk.
Those who talk do not know.
–*Tao Te Ching*

I taught law school for twenty years. The best class I ever taught was when I had laryngitis and couldn't even squeak for several days. We couldn't afford to cancel class and get behind, so I spent some time planning the class around group work. I typed out a series of steps that I wanted the groups to follow. When I walked into class, I smiled and silently handed out the instructions. At first, everyone just looked at me like maybe it was a joke and I would begin class in my usual way. Using hand gestures, I communicated that I wasn't kidding and urged them to begin.

As they worked, I walked around the class and eavesdropped. I was amazed at the creativity and productivity generated by the students as they set themselves to the task. It was like a treasure hunt for learning. The instructions were clues, and the students had to interpret them and find the treasure. There were furrowed brows and laughter. Ideas flew around the room like dragonflies. The students challenged and helped each other. At the end of class, they had accomplished more than assigned, and they were excited and pleased with themselves.

They learned a lot, but I learned even more. I learned that the less I spoke, the more they learned. It changed the way I taught.

Of course, during those days of involuntary silence, I couldn't talk at home either, much to my children's delight. It is amazing what your children will tell you when you can't talk back. When you can't correct or criticize or interrupt or command. Again, I learned. And it changed the way I parented.

Over the years, my voice has become more fragile. I get laryngitis from time to time. And if I yell, I quickly get hoarse. Although I missed cheering at my daughter's sporting events during her last high school years (I did lots of thumbs-up waving instead), I'm sure the kids didn't miss my angry yelling.

While I am prone to talking too much, I hope I am always becoming a better listener. I know I have learned more by biting my tongue than by spouting off about whatever I think I know.

> *The more you talk and think about it, the further astray you wander from the truth. Stop talking and thinking, and there is nothing you will not be able to know.*
>
> —SENG-TS'AN

The Mask of Happiness

In many situations, asserting our rightness is really about ego, or anger, or fear. In those situations, choosing to step back awakens compassion and brings inner peace and a sense of well-being. It keeps us connected to the other person in a genuine, loving way.

For example, suppose that your spouse is telling a story to friends and gets some of the peripheral details wrong. Is it better for you to correct these mistakes so that the story is accurate, or is it better to let the story continue, to let your spouse enjoy telling it, to let the listeners enjoy hearing it?

That's an easy one. Choosing to be right in that situation might cause embarrassment or irritation for your spouse, and perhaps discomfort for the listeners. Choosing to be happy allows everyone to enjoy the moment, including you.

But what if you are reluctant to disagree with your spouse because, if you do, your spouse is likely to criticize you or get angry? What if you tell yourself you are choosing to be happy, but you are really making the choice out of resentment or fear or even your own anger? That is not choosing happiness. That is a mask of happiness. It separates us from others and hurts our spirit because it is not true.

When I was a girl, I remember playing a game with a boy at my house. I was winning because I was more skilled at the game. My mother called me aside and told me to let him win because he was a boy. She said he would feel bad if he lost to a girl. I remember thinking that that was a bunch of you-know-what, but she was my mother, so I hesitated, unsure how to proceed.

When we say we want to choose happiness instead of rightness, we don't mean that we want to silence our own voice of truth. We don't mean that we want to keep the peace by betraying our spirit. It doesn't mean going along to be part of the crowd. It doesn't mean choosing fear.

> *Worse than telling a lie is spending your whole life staying true to a lie.*
> –ROBERT BRAULT

When Right Is Happy

The time is always right to do what is right.
–Martin Luther King Jr.

In this chapter, we have been focusing on making conscious decisions about when to assert our "rightness," and when to choose instead to be happy. For example, there was the waiter who corrected my pronunciation in the restaurant. Instead of letting it pass, I got huffy and corrected him right back. Scenarios like this often involve an ego that feels embarrassed or threatened.

Sometimes there is not really a right or wrong answer, just opinions. For example, one topic that generated a lot of strongly worded comments on my blog was whether the toilet paper should roll over the top or from underneath. And if people will argue about that, then how much more invested will they be about opinions that really matter? Our insistence on the rightness of our opinions often hinders respectful debate and prevents connection with those who think differently than we do.

The choice between being right and being happy invites us to explore our underlying assumptions about our own knowledge. Sometimes when I look beneath some unquestioned belief, I find that my foundation for that belief is not as concrete as I thought. I have, on rare occasions, even decided that I was mistaken. Or I have at least entertained the possibility, however unlikely, that I *could* be mistaken.

At the beginning of the chapter is a quote by General Patton: "Don't fight a battle if you won't gain anything by winning." In many scenarios, a quick cost-benefit analysis would suggest that the benefit of asserting our rightness does not outweigh the expense of our happiness or the happiness of others.

Does that mean that it is never right to be right? What about standing up against injustice? The Noble Eightfold Path is full of rightness—Right View, Right Intention, Right Speech, Right Action, Right Livelihood, Right Effort, Right Mindfulness, Right Concentration. Was Buddha wrong?

What do we really mean by deciding to be right or happy? Are these choices always mutually exclusive? Can they be reconciled?

It seems that when we explore this issue of being right or being happy from different angles, there are two kinds of "right."

There is the sense of right that is ego driven. This might manifest as self-righteousness, when we believe that our opinion is superior. Our egos might react to actual or perceived criticism with a defensive assertion of rightness. We might want to show off by correcting someone or displaying our knowledge about something. In many, if not all, of these situations, there is an underlying fear—fear of attack, fear of unworthiness, fear of embarrassment, fear of failure. The result is that we separate ourselves from others at the most basic level of our shared humanity. By insisting on our rightness, we cause the very isolation that we fear.

There is another sense of right that is driven by lack of ego. This manifests as integrity, honor, and courage. This is the rightness of the Noble Eightfold Path of Buddhism, the rightness of Gandhi, Martin Luther King Jr., Mother Teresa, Nelson Mandela. This is the rightness of the child who stands up to the bully on the playground, the homeless person who finds and returns a wallet full of money, a parent who admits a mistake to a child, a friend who honors a promise. In many, if not all, of these situations, there is an underlying peace, even joy. The result is that we connect ourselves to others at the most basic level of our shared humanity. By adhering to rightness, we cause the very union that we long for. In this way, as George Washington said, "Happiness and moral duty are inseparably connected."

> *For now I see through a glass darkly, but then face to face. Now I know in part, but then I will know fully, even as I am known.*
> —1 CORINTHIANS 13:12

P.S. And really, y'all know that the toilet paper should roll over the top!

Step 3

Give Up the Delusion of Control

God grant me the serenity to accept the things I cannot change
The courage to change the things I can
And the wisdom to know the difference.
　　　　　　　　　　　　　—REINHOLD NIEBUHR

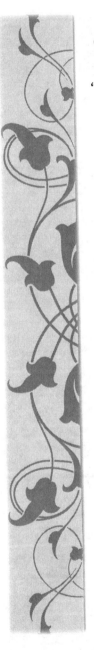

The Serenity Prayer might be the second most important prayer in the universe, second only to "thank you." Of all the 10 Steps, this one presented the greatest challenge to me. Trying to forcibly pry our fingers loose from our vise grip on control will only increase our panicked grasping, so we need to step back and take a breath. Developing the habit of letting go is impossible without understanding more about why we hold so tightly to our delusions. Let's take a look first at where that urge to control comes from. If we look with gentleness and understanding, our fingers will begin to relax and, like a toddler learning to walk, we will let go of the furniture long enough to take our first wobbly steps into freedom.

Man Plans, God Laughs

If you don't have children, you might still be under the delusion that you can control things. Children are God's cure for this. I think of children as God's twelve-step program for control addicts.

When I adopted my daughter, I consulted a friend who is a renowned astrologer. She contemplated Mia's chart and frowned. "Are you sure this is the correct birth date?" she asked. It was, as far as I knew. She started fidgeting, her eyes darting around the room as if looking for a quick escape. She stared at the chart as if willing it to change. She cleared her throat several times.

"What?!" I finally erupted, making her jump. "What is it?"

"Well," she said, desperate for some way to soften what she saw, "let's just say your daughter is... well, beyond programming."

Truer words were never spoken. That doesn't mean I didn't try. I had controlled things all my life. I thought I had to control things or things would not happen the way they were supposed to happen. But being in control required a lot of energy and vigilance. Eventually I wore myself out. Like a rock chip in a windshield, cracks lengthened and branched out over my delusion of control. Finally I asked myself, *What makes me think I know how things should happen?*

Here is one of my favorite passages. It's from *Another Roadside Attraction* by Tom Robbins:

Down by the waterfall, Amanda pitched her tent—it was made of willow sticks and the wool of black goats. Having filled the tent with her largest and softest paisley cushions, Amanda stripped down to her beads and panties and fell into a trance. "I shall determine how to prolong the lives of butterflies," she had previously announced.

However, an hour later when she awoke, she smiled mysteriously. "The life-span of the butterfly is precisely the right length," she said.

Over time I surrendered. I became wise in the ways of control. I had none. And it was good.

The Wisdom to Know the Difference

In the last line of the Serenity Prayer, we ask for the wisdom to know the difference between what we can and can't control. Although it comes at the end of the prayer, it seems like a good place to start.

At the beginning of one of my monthly discussion group meetings, we made two lists.

The first list was all the things we could not control: *kittens, weather, the economy, gravity, choices our children make, flight delays and cancellations, drunk drivers, earthquakes and other natural disasters, utilities getting interrupted, games of chance, what other people think of us, how other people react, whether our favorite sports team will win.*

The second list was all the things we could: *what we do or say or think.*

We concluded that the only things we can control are what we do or say or think, and that we can't control everything else. That's right, everything else. So now we have an easy way to determine the difference between what we can change and what we can't. We are very wise!

> *Yesterday I was clever, so I wanted to change the world.*
> *Today I am wise, so I am changing myself!*
> –Rumi

The Courage to Change the Things I Can

In a way, this whole book is about this second line of the Serenity Prayer, having the courage to change the things we can. Once we recognize our wisdom to know the difference between what we can change and what we can't, then any efforts we make to change can be directed at the one thing we can control: what we do or say or think.

But changing ourselves is often difficult. And scary. Indeed, I think many of our misguided efforts to change all those things outside of ourselves are based in fear, fear of looking in the mirror and taking responsibility for changing the only thing we can. Hence the prayer for courage.

I prayed a lot for courage the year two of my three daughters, still young and unmarried, surprised me with the news they were pregnant. I can tell you that there were many times along the way when I did not feel very brave. I wasn't very interested in changing me; I wanted to change them! Not just them, I wanted to change reality! But I knew enough by then to know that the only thing I had any control over was how I handled the situation through my thoughts and words and actions. And I knew that the choices I made then would set the tone for years to come.

By taking steps to acknowledge our responsibility for what we do and say and think, in big and small ways, we show courage. We are very brave!

When we are no longer able to change a situation,
we are challenged to change ourselves.
–Viktor E. Frankl

94

The Serenity to Accept
the Things I Cannot Change

If a problem has a solution, there is no need to worry.
If a problem has no solution, there is no need to worry.
—the Dalai Lama

Sometimes I think I am accepting something, but I don't feel serene. It's more like grumpy resignation. In the prayer, however, the serenity precedes the acceptance. Just as courage leads to change, and wisdom leads to discernment, serenity leads to acceptance. So the question is, how do we attain serenity?

My cousin sent me this true story about a bear rescued from a bridge.

The bear was walking across the Rainbow Bridge on Old Highway 40 in California. The bridge spans a dry gulch. Two cars crossing the bridge from opposite directions scared the bear, and it clambered over the side only to find itself on a narrow ledge with no way back up and no way down. Falling or jumping meant certain death on the rocks far below. Although authorities were called, they could do nothing, and they left the bear to its fate. The next day, they came back to see what had happened and found the bear sound asleep on the ledge. With renewed resolve, they rigged a net under the bear, tranquilized it, and lowered it to the ground, where it woke up and calmly walked away.

That bear was an enlightened Zen master.

A few days ago, I drove up to my cabin. There was a lot of snow, and the driveway to the cabin is not plowed, so I had to park a short distance away on a plowed road and walk in. As I was loading myself up like a donkey, I suddenly realized that my keys were not in my hand where they had been just moments before. I had not stepped more than a few feet away from the car, so they had to be close by. And yet, try as I might, I could not find them. Not in my pockets, not in the car, not on the ground, not in the bags I was carrying.

I was not calm like the bear. There I was on a gorgeous sunny winter day in the forest, the musical burbling of the creek nearby, and I was in a proper snit. I kept going over the same places again and again—pockets, car, ground, bags. No keys. I was self-aware enough to see that my emotional turmoil was not helping, but still...

Finally, I made one more pass over everything and walked on to the cabin, using the hidden key to get in. (Yes, I knew there was a spare key, and I still allowed myself to get frustrated!) After I put things away, I went down to the creek to contemplate the crack in the parallel universes that the keys had slipped through. Then I walked back to the car to have another look. And there the keys were, safely returned from the other universe, tucked down between the seat and the console.

All that agitation and panic did not contribute one tiny bit to finding the keys. Why is it that even when I know I can't control something, I still want to and even try to? Where does that urge to control, despite everything I rationally know, come from?

For me, it comes from fear. Fear blocks my serenity, so I need to address that fear before I can serenely accept anything. I need to look below that desperate desire to make things other than what they are, and find the terrors lurking in the dark corners.

In the meantime, I think I'll take a nap.

Embrace the nap!

—MY GRANDSON'S DADDY, TRYING TO CONVINCE AN ACTIVE,

OVER-TIRED BABY TO QUIET DOWN

It Is Not So

Go to the places that scare you.

—ADVICE FROM HER TEACHER TO THE TIBETAN YOGINI MACHIG LABDRÖN

Pema Chödrön told the story of a young warrior who had to battle fear. She did not want to fight, but her teacher insisted. On the day of battle, the warrior stood on one side, feeling small. Fear stood on the other side, looking big and wrathful. The warrior bowed to show respect and asked fear, "How do I defeat you?" Fear thanked her for showing respect and replied, "My weapons are that I talk fast and get in your face. Then you get completely unnerved, and you do whatever I say. If you don't do what I say, I have no power."

Sounds so simple. But when I am anxious or afraid, my instinct is to act, or rather, to react. I am tempted to listen to fear and engage on fear's terms. Fear is telling me to get away from the discomfort, the distress, the embarrassment, the shame. Fear tells me to fight, to close my heart, to run, to hide.

In tae kwon do, we have to spar. I'm not very good at it. I get anxious even though we are padded up like Pillsbury Doughboys and we don't use full contact, so I know I am not going to get injured. Still, my opponents are always younger and faster. When someone is throwing a kick at me, my instinct is to back away, but my reflexes are not what they used to be, so I usually lose the point. The teacher told me to move forward, toward my opponent, rather than away. Surprisingly, the safest place is right up close.

So it is with fear. Move close to fear. In *Dune*, the acclaimed sci-fi novel by Frank Herbert, character Paul recites a litany against fear:

> Fear is the mind killer. Fear is the little death that brings total obliteration. I will face my fear. I will permit it to pass over me and through me. And when it has gone past, I will turn the inner eye to see its path. Where the fear has gone, there will be nothing. Only I will remain.

Sometimes I actually say this to myself. Silly, I know, but it calms me. *A Course in Miracles* says that fear and love cannot coexist because fear is the perception, albeit erroneous, of the absence of love. When we are afraid, we experience separation and loneliness. I find great comfort in this loving passage: "One gently walks with you who answers all your fears with one merciful reply, 'It is not so.'"

So when fear is in my face talking fast, I take a deep breath and bow with respect. And then I look fear in the eye and say, "It is not so."

He who knows how to live can walk abroad
Without fear of rhinoceros or tiger.
He will not be wounded in battle.
For in him rhinoceroses can find no place to thrust their horn,
Tigers no place to use their claws,
And weapons no place to pierce.
Why is this so?
Because he has no place for death to enter.
−TAO TE CHING

Not Doing What Fear Tells Us to Do

When I am stressed or angry or afraid, when I am feeling out of control on the inside, my first instinct is to seek relief by trying to exert control on what is outside myself. Predictably, those efforts meet with little success, which in turn fuels my own suffering.

When I look at the fear, I see stories. My stories. I see that I tell myself stories about what is happening. These are not happy stories. I see that I am judging my circumstances as bad. I'm playing the what-if game by spinning out imagined scenarios of disaster, shame, disappointment, helplessness. As someone told me years ago, my brain is a scary place. And for most of my life, it was.

Once I understood that my suffering was of my own creation, that I was choosing to tell myself these stories, choosing to play the what-if game, I realized that I had the power to make a different choice. Telling myself these stories, playing the what-if game, was a habit, a habit that could be changed like any other habit.

Here are some of the ways I've shifted my habitual response to fear. The key is to find what works for you.

>*Change the story.* If we are telling ourselves a story full of dire scenarios, we can recognize that it is just a story. We can ask ourselves if we know for a fact that it is true. What other story could we tell ourselves? Or could we suspend all stories and just be with what is?

Question judgment. I try to remind myself that I don't know if a particular event is good or bad. What looks like a tragedy to me right now might turn out to be a magnificent blessing. The best example is my daughter Mia's unexpected pregnancy. What I initially judged as a devastating turn of events has turned out to be the best thing that ever happened to her. She is a responsible and loving mother, and that has helped her improve other areas of her life as well. If I had known, I would have been celebrating the news rather than grieving over it.

Look for inspiration. I find inspiration in poems, quotations, stories, and verses from the Bible or from other faith traditions that inspire trust in the basic goodness of the universe.

Make friends with fear. We fuel our fear by being afraid of it, by fighting it, by denying it. We can invite our demons to tea, engage our fear in conversation, be curious about it, get to know it, have compassion for it and for ourselves. Shine a light in the darkness. The unknown is much scarier than the known.

Take a nap! Like the bear stranded on the bridge, we can put aside our concerns and take a break. This is not the same as denial, which will never work (take my word for it!). But we can refresh ourselves with exercise, belly breathing, meditation, prayer, or whatever else we can do to rejuvenate our spirit.

If we can make peace with our fear, that urge to control will loosen its grip. Serenity is freed to well up. Acceptance flows naturally.

> *FEAR: False Evidence Appearing Real*
> –Unknown

Night of the Skunk

In her book *A Return to Love*, Marianne Williamson described a period of her life when she kept getting knocked to her knees by a series of life challenges. She would struggle to her feet only to be knocked down again. Finally it dawned on her that perhaps she should stay on her knees.

I've gone through times like that. Most of us have. I remember the night of the skunk. I was going through some tough times. I had a car accident and was seriously injured. While I was recovering from that, my dad had a heart attack and died. And during this time there were what seemed like almost daily setbacks of much smaller magnitude, but when you are dealing with major injuries and losses, even minor difficulties seem huge.

I tried to soldier on. I went back to work before I should have. I refused offers of help. I was determined to go on with my life as though everything were normal. But it was taking a toll. I was exhausted, physically and emotionally. I finally reached the end of my coping rope. I called a friend one evening and told her that I just wanted to go to bed for several months. Bed seemed like the only safe place where nothing could happen to me. I wanted to pull the covers over my head and hibernate until the world improved.

That very night I woke up suddenly. The room was pitch-black. There was a smell that I can't even begin to describe. I thought some hideous monster from hell was in the room with me. I reached for the light. And there, sitting on the bed, looking so pleased with themselves were my two dogs, who had obviously been on the wrong end of a skunk. (They had a dog door that allowed them to come and go between the house and the fenced backyard.) I quickly shooed them outside and then realized that the smell was on everything they had touched, so I pulled off the bed linens and blankets and threw them in the backyard, too, along with my nightclothes.

So I'm standing at the back door in the middle of the night, naked, and then I see that the skunk has not fared so well—it is dead in the back yard. Having to dispose of the skunk carcass was the final straw.

The night of the skunk. On my knees. I stayed there.

> *Suffering is the extra tension created in the mind*
> *when it struggles.*
> —SYLVIA BOORSTEIN

Word of the Year 2011

In the final minutes of New Year's Eve, I pick a word for the following year. It is always a verb. It is not a resolution. My word is a focus word, a gentle reminder, a guide. I write the word on little cards that I place where my gaze is sure to light: by my computer, next to the bathroom mirror, on the car dash. Throughout the year, my word is there, wherever I look. As the months go by, it becomes a part of me.

How do I choose my word? Sometimes I am pretty sure I know before New Year's Eve, but more often I don't. As the year comes to a close, I open my mind and heart. The word comes to me, like a whisper in my soul.

This is the word I chose for 2011: *yield*.

This word danced around my awareness for a few weeks before the end of the year. I thought it might be my word, but I wanted to keep my mind open. No other word came. By New Year's Eve, I knew *yield* was here to stay. As the word settled into my soul, here are some of the things I thought about.

What first came to mind were these line from the *Tao Te Ching*:

> Yield and overcome
> Bend and be straight

As I sat with the word, other meanings began to enter my thoughts, at first just in a trickle, but soon a stream:

A fertile field yields a bountiful harvest.
A branch yields to wind and does not break.
We yield the right of way.
We yield to God's will or to our inner wisdom.
We yield as a gesture of courtesy or respect.
We yield (or resist yielding!) to temptation.
We yield in surrender or defeat.

It was only the first minute of 2011, and I was already feeling a bit overwhelmed by my word. Then the word whispered again in my soul. *Yield.* I don't need to understand it all right now. I only need to...yield. Yield in faith. And so I do. I yield.

Let It Go, Crow!

While I was biding my time at a very long stoplight a while ago, I noticed a crow perched on the tippy-top spire of a tall, tall evergreen. Rather, trying to perch. The spindle was not strong enough, so every time the crow tried to settle, the branch would fold under its weight. The bird would flap frantically to keep from falling and then try to settle again.

I was so intrigued that after the light finally changed, I pulled to the side of the road where I could park and watch. Why didn't the bird just fly to one of the nearby trees or hop down to a sturdier branch? Did it think that apical sprig was suddenly going to solidify? I was reminded of the saying that insanity is doing the same thing over and over, thinking you will get a different result.

I could relate to that silly crow. How many times have I acted or reacted in some stubborn or habitual way, thinking that this time it would have the desired result? I can see my therapist sitting in her chair years ago, looking at me with the hint of a smile, asking, "And how is that working for you *now?*"

In fact, just three short days after I saw the crow, I saw my daughter starting to repeat a pattern that, in the past, has not led to happy results for her. I sighed and sat down at the table with her to comment on this. As soon as I started to speak, *she* sighed and did a subtle eye roll, but I caught it. This did not deter me. I shared my observations with her...as I have done every time before. And gave her my advice...as I have done every time before. Knowing that she would disregard it...as she has done very time before. And already feeling frustrated...as I have felt every time before.

Are y'all laughing yet?

> *Be like the bird, who*
> *Halting in her flight*
> *On limb too slight*
> *Feels it give way beneath her,*
> *Yet sings,*
> *Knowing she hath wings*
> *–Victor Hugo*

Roger That, Sparky!

Remember when Wendy finds Peter Pan in her room looking for his shadow? As she sews it back onto his feet, she chatters on until Peter scrunches up his face and says, "Girls talk too much!"

Well, I don't know that this is really a gender issue, but I do know that sometimes I talk too much, especially as a parent. I overexplain, repeat instructions and, yes, nag. When my son James was little, he would finally hold up his hand and say in a robot voice, "Talking is over." That used to crack me up.

What is all that too much talking about? I think it comes from anxiety, which triggers a need for control. And I tend to seek control with words. Someone once observed that my weapon of choice is a telephone. I also have long been the family member or friend who writes official letters. I am a negotiator by profession. I use words to achieve some desired end.

That can be a good thing, sometimes. But not so good when I use words to stifle someone else's words, to take up too much space in the conversation, to silence opposition, to distrust someone else's competence, to deny my own uncertainty, to win.

A while back, I was helping my daughter Grace write a cover letter for a job application. The job was one I encouraged her to apply for, and I did a little networking on her behalf to ensure that her application would at least get considered. I knew Grace was excited about the opportunity, and I also knew that when she gets excited or anxious, Grace can sometimes become immobilized instead of following through.

I set out clear expectations (mine) that she would send the letter off right away. And shortly after that, I sent her a text message urging her again not to delay. I knew I was being pushy, that I was getting myself invested in what was really her business, but I couldn't seem to let it go.

Grace would have been well within her rights to tell me at this point to back off. But instead of expressing irritation, she sent this reply text message: *Roger that, Sparky!* Sparky is Grace's special name for me. I don't remember when she started using it or why, but it stuck. She doesn't use it all the time, but when she does, it carries much affection and always makes me smile.

When I got the text, I laughed and relaxed. Grace was acknowledging that she heard me loud and clear. She would follow through...or not. But it was out of my hands. Since then, I have caught myself several times just at the edge of talking too much. I smile to myself and think, *Roger that, Sparky!* And let it go.

> *I think I must let go. Must fear not, must be quiet*
> *so that my children can hear the Sound of Creation*
> *and dance the dance that is in them.*
> —RUSSELL HOBAN

As It Is

Expectations destroy our peace of mind, don't they? They're
future disappointments planned out in advance.
—Elizabeth George

I remember when a professional first assessed James as autistic.
He was four years old. A few days later, as I was still trying to take
that in, terrified about what it meant for my son and what it meant
for me, feeling disoriented and desperate and in denial, a friend's
mother asked me, "So how do you feel about the fact that James
won't be going to Harvard?"

All these years later, I still marvel at her insensitivity. But that is
not the point here. The point is that I did have expectations, perhaps not of Harvard, but of what life would be like for my son, what
life would be like for me as his mother.

I did not relinquish those expectations without a fight. I fought
for years. I fought for the hopes and dreams and fantasies I was so
attached to that I couldn't imagine what life would be like if I gave
them up. I fought so hard to get away from what was real that I
caused a lot of unnecessary pain—to myself, to James, and to others.

On the outside, I was being a good advocate for James. I tried
every possible therapy, took advantage of every special ed service,
consulted with an array of experts, and read a library full of books.
But on the inside I was simply trying to escape, to escape the pain

of loving my child so fiercely and so helplessly. I was trying to make reality something other than what it was. In retrospect, I think my denial and my efforts to control something I couldn't control caused me more suffering that the autism itself.

Expectations are not really bad. We should hope for and anticipate things. When we make goals, we strive to attain them. We expect certain outcomes to result from certain efforts. But when our expectations do not come to pass, we are sad.

Then sometimes we increase and prolong our suffering because of our attachment to our expectations, our unwillingness to acknowledge that things did not turn out the way we wanted, our quickness to blame someone or something, our refusal to grieve and move on.

Last year, I had expectations. I had plans and hopes and dreams and fantasies, all of which brought me considerable delight in anticipation. I was getting ready to retire, and I had plans for what I had designated as the Year of Me. I also had hopes and dreams for my kids, all of whom had finally graduated from high school and entered young adulthood. I was going to reclaim my own independent adult life. I saw the light at the end of the tunnel. Little did I know it was a train! Two of my three daughters blindsided me with the news they were pregnant. But this time I was better prepared than when James was little.

Yes, among the many feelings roiling around in my spirit in those first weeks were anger and resentment. Understandably, some would say. I would say, too. However, while honoring those feelings, I knew at the same time that they did not serve my well-being or the well-being of my children. I knew that I had choices to make about what I wanted for myself, for my relationship with my daughters, for my relationship with my grandchildren. I knew that the choices I made right then would have consequences long into the future. I wanted to choose wisely.

So I went up to my cabin to be with my feelings, to meditate and pray, to search my heart, to listen to the creek. I saw that underneath my anger, one thing I was struggling with was my lack of control. I was losing something I had looked forward to and I had no control over what was happening.

I took out some paper and wrote a description of what my life would have been like if things had gone as planned. Some of the things I had planned were still possible, so I didn't include those. I only wrote about what I was sure I was losing. Of course, I was writing about a future not yet here, and no one knows what really would have happened, but I assumed that everything would have gone according to plan, my plan. I wrote out my wildest fantasies of blissful retirement. Everything was exactly the way I wanted. It was glorious. Then I sat with that paper. I read my fantasies out loud. I said how much I would miss them. I cried over them. I wished them well. I gently placed the paper in the fire and offered my broken dreams to the heavens.

Acknowledging and honoring my feelings allowed me to release the anger and resentment. As the fire burned the paper, it burned off the crust of hardness on my heart, and the smoke carried the spirit-choking toxins up the chimney.

In the emptiness left behind, I felt something emerging alongside the sadness. Love. Deep deep love for my daughters, for the children they were carrying, and for myself. And excitement. I was going to be a grandmother. More than all my fantasies of what might have been, I knew I wanted to be present for what was. I wanted to be present for my own life. I wanted to be present for my children and for their children. I wanted to face a new beginning.

So when you feel all the endings coming ... begin looking for all the beginnings.
  —ANN VOSKAMP

Bloom Where You're Planted

I had the good fortune to live overseas in three different countries with very different cultures. In two of these countries, I helped form professional women's groups to share information and experiences. One group grew to have over 150 members from over thirty countries. Meeting all these interesting women and hearing their stories was one of the highlights of my expatriate life. Out of these stories, two themes emerged.

First, almost all of those of us who were employed had gotten our jobs through networking, especially with other women. When we operated as a community, all of us were less isolated and more successful. Because of the practical and emotional support we received through networking, we made a decision to keep the group as open as possible so that we could be a resource for as many women as possible. The term *professional* was used only to distinguish the group from those that were organized primarily for social or charitable purposes. The door was open to any woman who wanted to participate. No one was excluded.

Looking back, that was an important lesson that shaped my future. I learned that my life is enriched when I don't set prerequisites for who is "qualified" to be in my life. I learned that all the differences we perceive between ourselves and others (cultures, professions, faiths, experiences, opinions) expand our lives when we view each other with genuine interest and goodwill rather than with judgment and fear. And I learned that underneath those differences, we really are all the same.

Second, almost all of us were working at things other than what we were trained to do. A scientist was an author, a nurse was a consultant, a homemaker was an expert on local crafts, and a former Playboy bunny was an antiques dealer (no kidding).

This second theme was a surprise to all of us, so we tried to understand why so many of us shared this common experience of working outside of our original fields. We realized that most of us came into our new environments with certain labels—I am a businesswoman; I am a lawyer; I am a stay-at-home mom; I am a teacher—that became restrictive as we tried to find a place for ourselves in our new country. When we dropped the labels and were able to focus instead on our talents and interests, our self-identities became more fluid. We were able to recognize new opportunities that had been obscured by our rigid labels.

This wasn't always easy. Many of us had a lot invested in our identities, including money, time, and hard work. These labels were marks of pride and accomplishment. And security. Dropping them meant leaving our comfort zones. There was disappointment and anxiety. But there was also liberation. And growth. And new confidence. Those of us who were able to let go found that we not only thrived but also were happier.

Another important lesson. We can't always control the circumstances we find ourselves in. But if we can let go of expectations and use the resources at hand, we can bloom where we're planted. And if we can bloom where we're planted, then wherever we're planted will become our happy place.

We must be willing to let go of the life we have planned, so as to accept the life that is waiting for us.
—JOSEPH CAMPBELL

Grace Under Fire

Grace joined our family when she was fourteen. She was beautiful and funny and good hearted, but she was in foster care for a reason, which meant that she had "issues." I call Grace my alpha child because she was used to being in charge. Although she was not the oldest in our household, she was the most forceful, and she quickly dominated the other children. I was often saying, "Grace, that is not your job. I am the only parent in this house."

I believed that with a safe and stable home, Grace would flourish. I believed that she would be integrated into the family. What I really believed above all else was that I could make all this happen. By using excellent parenting methods. By sheer force and consistency of will. By unconditional love. Any experienced social worker, teacher, or parent reading this is laughing out loud by now.

Everyone will be laughing once you read this: I was already raising three kids, including two with autism, by the time Grace joined our family. Why did I still think I had any control? I could not fix James's autism. Mia was "beyond programming," as the astrologer had warned me. And Dan was... Dan was sort of like a teenage sprite from another galaxy (think Mork). But I am a stubborn and determined problem solver, and with each new challenge, I still clung to the belief that I could control my world.

Grace was a one-person twelve-step program. She was the one who got me to admit that I was powerless and that my life had become unmanageable. Because of her, I made a decision to turn my life over to my higher power. *Please take it!* I sank to my knees in surrender and stayed there.

Miracles happen when you are not in control. Grace chose to leave our home, and I had to let her go. But she came back. Now she is a loved (she always was that) and loving part of the family. All I really had to do was get out of God's way. As a friend of mine often says, "Thank God I'm not in control of my life!"

On my knees. In gratitude.

For peace of mind, resign as general manager of the universe.
                                                    –UNKNOWN

The Doors of Change

Beginnings are such fragile times.
–Frank Herbert

In *Open the Door,* author Joyce Rupp used a door as a symbol of spiritual growth. In one chapter she quoted a poem written by a twelve-year-old girl named Mary Katherine Lidle. The day after she wrote this poem, Mary was killed in a car accident. Here is the last part of the poem.

> Listen to me
> Go through those doors with hope
> Go through those doors knowing change is the future and
>   you're part of it
> You don't know what change is; that's why you're scared
> Change is the sun booming over the horizon
> Scattering rays of hope to a new day
> Change is a baby lamb meeting the world for the first time
> Change is growing from a young child to a young woman
> Change is beautiful; you will learn to love it

I wonder if Mary's spirit knew her life was going to change dramatically the next day. Did she write this poem to leave some comfort for her grieving family? Where did these words come from to be written by a twelve-year-old girl on the last day of her life?

Doors. Doors closing. Doors opening. Sometimes our urge to control is about trying to make things different than they are. But just as often, our urge to control is about keeping things the same. Like it or not, change happens. In ways that we can foresee and in ways we never saw coming. I retired last year. That was planned change. Two of my daughters had babies. That was a surprise. In moments when I move through the fear, I breathe in serenity and accept the unfolding, the uncertainty around the bend, the beauty of beginnings. I am learning to love it.

> *Man cannot discover new oceans unless he has*
> *the courage to lose sight of the shore*
> –André Gide

Step 4

Feel Your Feelings

First when there's nothing
but a slow glowing dream
that your fear seems to hide
deep inside your mind.
All alone I have cried
silent tears full of pride
in a world made of steel,
made of stone.
Well, I hear the music,
close my eyes, feel the rhythm,
wrap around, take a hold
of my heart.
What a feeling.
Bein's believin'.
I can have it all, now I'm dancing for my life.
Take your passion
and make it happen.
Pictures come alive, you can dance right through your life.
—"What a Feeling"

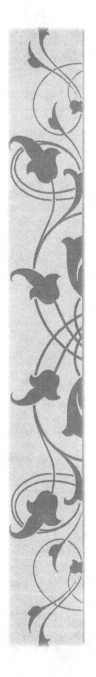

The first thing to know about feelings is that we have them. That might sound too obvious for words, but I spent so much of my life denying mine that I had to start at this very basic level. Feelings were big, dark, scary things that threatened to run amok and overwhelm me if not kept under tight control. And we know from the last step how well that control thing works!

Instead of barring the door against feelings, we can develop a habit of answering when they knock. Invite them in. Get to know them. Have some tea and cookies.

Nice to Meet You

The things you left behind will always find you in the future.
—Nikhil Anubhav Minz

What does feeling all of our feelings have to do with finding our happy place? As a former queen of denial, I can tell you that denying any feelings results in denying all feelings. And feelings will not be denied forever. They will find a way to manifest—in other feelings, in behaviors, in our minds, in our bodies. You have to admire them for their tenacity and confidence. Feelings are the best model we have of self-esteem. They demand respect.

When I lived in Thailand, I was impressed by how many words for feelings the Thai language offers. There are gradations and shades and nuances that are not available in English. Because language is so connected to our perception of ourselves and our world, it seems to me that the Thai people are very aware of feelings in themselves and others. They know their feelings much better than we English speakers do.

Does that make them happier? Eric Weiner thinks so. In his book *The Geography of Bliss*, he recounted his search for the happiest places in the world, including Thailand, known as the land of smiles. Along with many words for feelings, the Thais also have many words in their language for different kinds of smiles. Interesting, don't you think?

What we can learn about our feelings? Let's start by becoming acquainted with them. Some of us go through our lives without giving much attention to our feelings. Most of the time, we don't even know what we're feeling.

This was a challenge for me at an earlier time in my life. My therapist was a real stickler for feelings awareness. I would often start a sentence by saying, "I feel like..." She would stop me right there, encouraging me to identify an actual feeling. For example, if I said I felt like bolting right out of her office, she would suggest I say instead that I felt angry or afraid or sad or confused or fill-in-the-blank.

For those of you who are Thai or who know what you're feeling all the time, this probably sounds silly, but it was a big shift for me. I even had a list of feelings in case I needed some help. You can find lots of these lists online. The most extensive list I found, pages long, was on a marriage website. No coincidence there, I'm thinking.

Sometimes I pause and do a quick feeling inventory. What am I feeling right now? How do I experience those feelings in my body? If I'm feeling angry, maybe my heart is beating faster, my teeth are clenched, and I'm breathing more shallowly. If I'm feeling happy, my breathing might be more relaxed, and my face is smiling. I'm offering my feelings a positive check-in, a quick howdy. *Irritation, what's up? Contentment, nice to see you. Anger, roaring like a lion, I see. Excitement, what fun. Sadness, let's sit down.*

Once we become acquainted with our feelings, then we can get to know them better and improve our relationship with them through good habits. But just shaking hands with our feelings is a good start. With a smile.

The best and most beautiful things in the world cannot be seen or even touched. They must be felt with the heart.
–HELEN KELLER

Owning Our Feelings

"You make me so...!"

All of us have probably said this at one time or another. Probably more than once. Possibly many times. Because the saying really does seem true. Someone does something, and we feel pleased or upset. Our minds attach a causal connection between another's action and our feelings. But here's the key that can be tricky to grasp: Our feelings are based on our thoughts and beliefs. It is our thoughts about someone else's action that give rise to our feelings, not the act itself.

Attributing to someone or something else the power to make us feel a certain way leaves us helpless and passive. We see our feelings as an automatic response to outer stimuli we can't control. We are at the mercy of other people and events. We become feeling victims.

We can shift from being feeling victims to being feeling victors by a simple shift in language. Instead of saying, for example, "You make me so angry," say, "I feel angry." Own it. Consider the difference between the two. How do you feel when you say one or the other?

When I say, "You make me feel so...," I feel powerless and anxious, regardless of the feeling in the blank. I want you to behave a certain way so that I will feel a certain way. My emotional well-being is in your power, and I become dependent on you. If I'm feeling happy, good for you. If I'm not feeling happy, it must be your fault. Chances are I won't feel happy all the time, so I'm setting you up to fail. Even when I feel happy, there is always an underlying anxiety because I know I can't control your behavior. It will only be a matter of time before you do something to "cause" a distressing feeling.

When I say, "I feel...," I feel grounded and centered, even if the feeling itself is distressing. Owning my feeling gives me the opportunity to examine my underlying thoughts and beliefs and to adjust them if appropriate. I recognize my power to transform my feelings. Even distressing feelings are less scary because I have tools for dealing with them.

One of the greatest gifts we can give our children is to liberate them from being responsible for our feelings, and to help them learn to own their own feelings.

For example, my daughter related to me a conversation she had with her boyfriend, in which he blamed her for his feeling so stressed. We talked about how she was not responsible for his feelings and that his stress was his issue to grapple with. She felt vindicated and pleased that she could not be rightly blamed for his stress. Then she added, "He makes me so mad when he blames me for his feelings!"

Sigh.

Owning our feelings gives us a chance, a real chance, to alleviate our suffering instead of waiting for the world to make us happy.

Owning your own feelings, rather than blaming them on someone else, is the mark of a person who has moved from contracted to expanded awareness.
—DEEPAK CHOPRA

Mad/Sad/Glad Game

We fear violence less than our own feelings.
–Jim Morrison

My son James has autism. People with autism have difficulty with feelings. They don't pick up cues about what other people are feeling. They sometimes don't know what they are feeling themselves.

When James was a little boy, we would play the mad/sad/glad game. He would say mad or sad or glad, and then I would act out the feeling. If he said sad, I would make a very sad face and act like I was crying. I would say, "Oh, I feel so sad." Then he would name another feeling, and I would act it out with all the exaggerated drama I could muster. Then we would switch—I would name the feeling, and he would act it out. We only used those three. It was simple, and he liked words that rhymed. He loved the game, and we would play it over and over. I hoped that he would learn about his own feelings. I hoped that he would develop empathy for other people.

I look back at those years and realize that as I was trying so hard to help him understand feelings, I was denying mine. I felt so desperate. So alone. So terrified. Inadequate. Overwhelmed. Devastated. Ashamed. And angry. But I didn't acknowledge any of these feelings. As Jeff Lindsay observed, "I did not like this feeling of having feelings." They were terrifying. It was like having monsters locked in my basement. I kept them at bay by trying to "fix" my son.

How ironic. And futile. On both counts. My son is still autistic, and my monsters broke out long ago. I made my peace with them, and they moved on, although sometimes I still hear a few little ones scurrying around in the dark corners of the basement.

> *But feelings can't be ignored, no matter how unjust*
> *or ungrateful they seem.*
> —ANNE FRANK

The Book I Cannot Write

I spoke at a fund-raiser for Edwards Center, an organization that serves adults with developmental disabilities, like my two sons, who live in one of the organization's group homes and work at one of their sheltered work sites. I spoke about trying so hard for so many years to find a cure for James's autism... and failing. I spoke about becoming a foster parent to Dan when Dan's parents died and there was no foster family qualified to take him because of his autism. I spoke about being a single mother with two autistic teenagers, knowing that, like Dan's parents, I would be gone one day, and how terrified I was about what would happen to them then.

I spoke about sleeping easier these days knowing that they have a good life in the care of Edwards Center. They work and go out with friends and do everything that anyone else does, with the help of caring and trained staff. I see them most every week, unless they are too busy. They are thriving.

I spoke about hope. I hope I have done the best I can. I hope that Dan's mother looks down from heaven and believes that I have honored my promise to her to care for her son. I hope they are going to be all right when I'm gone.

It was a speech of joy and triumph, and immense gratitude. Yet when I spoke, my throat closed up and my eyes filled with tears. My voice quavered , and more than once I had to pause and take a deep breath. The sadness is never very far away.

I've learned that denying my sadness over the years, being afraid of the enormity and intensity of my feelings, not only deadened the pain but also deadened the joy. The First Noble Truth of Buddhism is that life is suffering. Our natural instinct is to avoid suffering, to run from it, to escape from it. But we can't. As Robert Frost observed, "The best way out is often through." When my pain eventually broke through, when I got too soul sick to fight anymore, I discovered that the released pain brought with it into the light the exquisite joy of life, here for us in unlimited abundance, always.

I write about James and Dan on my blog, as I have in this book, little snippets of the story that began over twenty-five years ago and will continue all my life, and theirs. People tell me I should write a book about parenting autistic children, that it would help other parents. Perhaps it would. But it is a book I cannot write. Perhaps because writing little pieces of the story here and there, as I do, does not ask me to leave the present to revisit those dark and deadened times for the extended periods that a book would require.

I've made my peace with sorrow. It doesn't go away, but it isn't scary anymore. I recognize it as the key to unlocking compassion. And compassion is the key to sweet, sweet happiness. Touching that raw place breaks my heart wide open, every time. And in that broken-open place, is a deep, deep well, a bottomless well of love.

The ideal of warriorship is that the warrior should be sad and tender, and because of that, the warrior can be very brave as well.
—CHÖGYAM TRUNGPA RINPOCHE

Inviting the Demons to Tea

Civilized people don't feel.
–MERVYN PEAKE

Mervyn Peake is my kind of guy. Feelings can be a downright nuisance. I've been out of sorts all week. Emo, as my daughter would say. Or at least I think that is what she would say. I'm still not sure exactly what that means. Quick to be irritated, quick to get teary. Restless, not sleeping. Even when I can shift to a better mood, I quickly sink back into my funk.

This morning I realized that all week I have been fighting my feelings instead of feeling my feelings. I relaxed my resistance and surrendered to my feelings, whispering, "This, too. This, too." No judgment. Just a soft opening. Unacknowledged grief blossomed. My foster daughter's beloved grandmother died Valentine's Day morning. My cousin died yesterday. Valentine's Day is also the day my dad died years ago. And my dog is getting old. Loss, memory of loss, anticipated loss. This, too. Grief wrapped me up like a soft down comforter. I snuggled in and rested.

Feelings are like water. We can try to dam them up, but they are purest when allowed to flow freely. Dammed-up feelings exert pressure, seek release. It takes a tremendous amount of energy to maintain that dam.

Milarepa, an eighth-century Tibetan Buddhist, returned to his cave one day to find it filled with demons. He tried to drive them out. They laughed at him. He tried to teach them Buddhism. They ignored him. He got angry and attacked them. They just yawned. Finally, he gave up and said, "I'm not going anywhere, and it seems that you are not either. I guess we will have to live here together. I'll make some tea," at which point the demons promptly left.

Living in your happy place doesn't mean always feeling happy. But it does mean honoring your feelings with gentle acceptance. All your feelings. This, too.

Which Wolf Are You Going to Feed?

It took me years to value acknowledging and honoring my feelings rather than denying them or repressing them. But some people have no problem identifying their feelings. On the contrary, their feelings are front and center, out of control, buffeting, raging, exhausting. How do we honor our feelings and at the same time not be at their mercy?

There is a story about a Native American boy who was angry and upset, and went to his grandfather for advice. The grandfather told him, "I have two wolves inside my heart. One of them is kind and understanding. He lives in harmony and peace. The other wolf is vengeful and cruel. He rages, but his anger changes nothing. The two wolves fight inside me to see which is more powerful." The boy asked his grandfather which wolf would win the fight in his heart. The grandfather responded, "The one I feed."

I have read that the natural lifespan of any emotion is one and a half minutes, just ninety seconds. After that, we need to give it more energy to keep it going. We need to feed it. This gives "nursing a grudge" a whole new meaning.

We feed an emotion by attaching to it, telling ourselves stories about it, playing out scenarios based on it, nourishing it with our attention. Many of these represent habitual patterns. We often feed our negative feelings without even being aware of it. People sometimes refer to them as cognitive distortions, a term that sounds a bit like a space-time anomaly from Star Trek. Do any of these sound familiar?

Overgeneralization: We see a single event as a never-ending pattern. If two of your favorite words are *always* and *never*, this one's yours!

Filtering: We pick out a single negative detail and amplify it while discounting positive details. Over twenty years of teaching, I accumulated a treasure trove of lovely and gracious and appreciative evaluations from students. Which is the one comment that I've never forgotten? The one that said I should never be allowed to teach that course again! Good grief. Do you ever lie in bed replaying the one thing that went wrong that day instead of all the things that went right?

Mind reading: We guess what someone is thinking and react accordingly. For a long time after two of my daughters surprised me with the news that they were pregnant, I felt embarrassed. I assumed that people were judging me as a bad mom and my daughters as bad girls. Maybe some people did. But certainly not all people, as I thought, against all reason.

Forecasting: We anticipate that things will turn out badly without any legitimate grounds for believing so. I've done a lot of that with my kids. The first time I let Mia ride her bike around the block—a small block in a safe residential area with smooth sidewalks—I just about had a heart attack imagining all the terrible things that might happen after she turned the corner and was out of sight for, oh let's say, about ninety seconds. It seemed like hours! By the time she came back into view, laughing and so proud of herself, I was poised to dial 9-1-1. My heart still beats faster just thinking about it, and that was over ten years ago. Lord, help me.

A telltale sign of forecasting are questions that begin with "What if...?" If forecasting were an Olympic event, I would have a wall of gold medals.

Magnification or minimization: We exaggerate the importance of things, like thinking we are terrible parents because we let our children watch TV one evening, or (horrors) more than one evening. Or we inappropriately shrink the significance of something, such as dismissing abusive or bullying behavior. I am quick to see this behavior when directed toward others, but in the past often overlooked it when it was directed at me.

Personalization: We see ourselves as the cause of some negative external event for which we were not primarily responsible. This one has my name written all over it. I held myself responsible for my mother's headaches. Well, okay, maybe some of those really were my fault. Just kidding. Sort of. I somehow believed that my son's autism was my fault, as was my failure to find a cure for him. Children often see themselves as the center of the universe, which is terrifying. I think this childhood distortion carried over to much of my adult life

In fact, I can relate to each of these. Yep, every one. Do any of these sound familiar to you? These ways that we feed our feelings become habits, thinking habits. Once we are aware of them, we can change them by changing our thoughts. Simple, right?

> *Whatever is true, whatever is noble, whatever is right,*
> *whatever is pure, whatever is lovely, whatever is*
> *admirable — if anything is excellent or praiseworthy —*
> *think about such things.*
> —Philippians 4:8

Transforming Our Feelings

If you are distressed by anything external, the pain is not due
to the thing itself but to your own estimate of it; and this
you have the power to revoke at any moment.
–MARCUS AURELIUS

In Step 3, we learned that the only things we can control are our thoughts, words, and actions. What about our feelings, too? The answer to that is no...and yes.

Have you ever heard or spoken these words, to yourself or to others? *Don't worry. Stop being so sad. Be happy. Please don't be angry.* Even the Bible says, "Fear not." I haven't had much success with controlling feelings. The phrase *herding cats* comes to mind. At best, my efforts to bring my feelings to heel simply ended in denial or repression.

But look below the feelings and you will find thoughts. Unlike feelings, we can choose our thoughts. If we can change our thoughts, we change our feelings. I like this approach because it honors our feelings rather than denying or repressing them.

The Dalai Lama himself uses this method of cognitive intervention to replace anxiety-generating thoughts with well-reasoned positive thoughts. The method goes by several names, such as CBT (cognitive behavior therapy) and REBT (rational emotive behavior therapy) and can be described as recasting or rewriting the story. You can search online for those to get worksheets that will lead you through a series of questions:

1. Trigger: What happened that caused an emotional reaction?
2. Feelings: What feelings am I experiencing? How intense are they?
3. Beliefs: What went through my mind? What beliefs do I have about this event?
4. Evaluation: Do I know for a fact that these beliefs are true? Am I playing head games (amplifying, guessing, identifying, forecasting, blaming, justifying)?
5. Alternatives: Is it possible that other or opposite beliefs are true? Is there another way of seeing this?
6. Feelings: What am I feeling now that I've considered other beliefs?

I have run through this list of questions in many circumstances. If a distressing feeling is particularly intense and recurring, I have to repeatedly ask myself the questions, as I describe in the next section.

Emotions don't reveal the quality of your life; they reveal the quality of your thinking at any particular moment.
−TOMMY NEWBERRY

I Love a Parade!

If you are getting run out of town, get in front
and make it look like a parade.
–Unknown

A while back, something happened that threw me for a loop. Someone near and dear to me was behaving in ways I could not understand. I tried hard to be supportive, but my efforts seemed to exacerbate the situation. When communication ceased, my feelings were deeply hurt. I struggled with how I was reacting. I felt angry and misunderstood and unappreciated. I felt confused and upside down, like I had been knocked over by a sneaker wave. Old habits beckoned like the Sirens luring sailors to shipwrecks on the rocky shore.

I wanted to lash out with righteous fury. I wanted the person who hurt me to be sorry. I wanted other people to sympathize with me. I was feeding the wolf a whole buffalo. I was blaming and judging. I was separating myself from the other person through my negative reaction. Fear blossomed like nightshade.

I was at least able to refrain from outwardly reacting while I sorted things out. I sat with my feelings and tried to breathe into them. I knew I did not like the way I was handling the situation, but I was hooked. Our feelings are our feelings—we can't order them about. So I went down a level.

I used what I knew about looking beneath the feelings for underlying thoughts and beliefs. What I discovered was lots of blaming, beliefs that I had made irreparable mistakes and that the other person was being deliberately punishing; judgment, believing that the other person was being deceptive, stubborn, inconsiderate, selfish, and ungrateful; and fear, believing that the other person would not resume communication, that we would never have a chance to work it out and that, even if we had a chance, our misunderstanding was too great to overcome.

Was it possible that there were other explanations for the interrupted communication? Yes. I felt my vice grip on anticipated disaster begin to loosen. Was it possible that we would be able to talk about this in the future? Yes. Panic began to subside. Was it possible that I would survive even if I didn't get the outcome I wanted? Yes. I rediscovered my basic trust in the universe. Was it possible that this other person had needs and concerns of which I was not aware? Yes. The beginning of empathy. Was it possible that this other person just didn't know how to come talk to me about these things? Yes. A glimmer of compassion.

Going through the process helped me recenter. I didn't know how things would develop, but my heart was not afraid, and I was reconnected to the caring I felt for the other person.

I was able to make this shift completely without any outside intervention. It was not dependent on what anyone else did or said. I could transform my feelings to soothe my fear and calm my distress. What I discovered was the calm after the storm.

And in that calm, all things are possible.

Cradling Our Feelings

Hush, little baby, don't you cry
Mama's gonna sing you a lullaby.
–"Hush, Little Baby"

Soon after I moved to the Northwest, my son James was diagnosed with autism.

Suddenly not only did I have a new home—I was in a new world, a world I did not want to be in. A world I didn't know how to navigate. A world I wanted only to escape from.

There were lots of people to meet that I otherwise never would have crossed paths with: Medical specialists. Education specialists. Support groups. I was flooded with way too much information. I couldn't begin to sort it out. I was numb. No time for feelings. I had to function. I was alone with a son I loved who had a problem.

Someone said I should talk to Sherry, a mom/expert. Sort of the mother superior for all the novitiate moms. I took James to her house. She was so friendly. I thought she was happy because she knew how to make this all go away. She was going to share the secret cure with me. She had this great big smile on her face as she exclaimed, "I love autism!" *Wow,* I thought, *will I ever love autism?* I was pretty sure I wouldn't.

We sat at her kitchen table while James played with her son. She was perky as she laid out the future, my future, and told me what I needed to do. I stared out the window, wanting to be anywhere but there. At one point Sherry was talking about another family. She sighed, shaking her head, and confided that they had not even grieved yet. Grief. Now there was a concept I had not thought of. She seemed to think that it was important. I filed that away for another day, another year, another decade.

Feelings can be so scary. Grief, anger, shame, sadness. Sometimes feelings are too scary to even name. But acknowledging our feelings can help us accept them. Labeling them brings them into the light. Tara Brach described the following example in her book *Radical Acceptance*. An elderly Buddhist teacher named Jacob continued to instruct even though he had midstage Alzheimer's. He sat down to teach a large group one time and suddenly couldn't remember why he was there. He began to panic. His training kicked in, and he started labeling out loud what was happening—afraid, confused, shaking, lost. Gradually, he relaxed, and he labeled that, too. Relaxed, safe, okay, calm. The students were moved to tears by this deep teaching. By simply labeling, he stayed grounded and didn't get sucked into his agitation.

Thich Nhat Hanh teaches us to cradle our feelings, all our feelings, like a baby. If you are agitated or overwhelmed by whatever you are feeling, you can label it like Jacob did. Then hold it gently in your arms and rock it like a baby. You can even rock your fear to sleep. I just had this image of Rosemary, in *Rosemary's Baby*, cradling her demon-spawn child. Love is that powerful. Cradling our feelings helps us contain them, tolerate them, soothe them, embrace them.

In a classic Buddhist story, a mother, crazed with grief over her son who just died, begs Buddha to use his power to bring her child back to life. Buddha promises her that he will grant her wish if she can bring him a mustard seed from a home in which no one has ever died. She frantically goes from door to door, but everyone tells her a story of loss. She cannot find even one home that has not been touched by death. By the time she returns to Buddha, she understands the truth of sorrow and life. She asks Buddha to help her bury her son and becomes his disciple.

When I feel a distressing feeling now, I think about all the other people in the world who feel this feeling. I know that whatever I feel has been felt before, and is being felt this very moment by millions of people. I reach out to them, filled with compassion for us all. Our hearts are one. And in that oneness I find peace. Living with the fear of feelings is much, much worse that living with the feelings themselves.

Now I know I've got a heart, 'cause it's breaking.
–THE TIN MAN, IN *THE WIZARD OF OZ*

Sabaay

When I lived in Thailand, I learned enough Thai to carry on a simple conversation. One thing that struck me about the Thai language was how many words they have for feelings, many more words than we have in English. I might say I feel annoyed but, in Thai, there are different words for the annoyance you feel when someone is late, when your cable service is interrupted during a key play in the game, or when a mosquito is buzzing around your ear.

The key role that feelings play is reflected in the typical Thai greeting, *Sabaay dii mai kha?* Loosely translated, this means, "Are you comfortable?" But the word *sabaay* means more than physical comfort. It includes the more subtle level of emotional comfort, or well-being. There is no adequate translation in English.

This concept of sabaay permeates everything and is central to all communication. In a language that has no word for a simple, blunt no, Thai is geared to creating and maintaining an environment of sabaay. This can lead to some misunderstanding with Westerners such as me, who value directness and depend on the technical precision of words, without regard to, or even awareness of, the subtle levels of emotional communication going on beneath the words.

As a contract negotiator, I learned much more from my Thai colleagues than they learned from me. I learned to listen between the lines, to hear what was not being said, to understand beyond the words. I carry many treasured memories of my years in Thailand. If you came to my house, you would see my love for that country reflected in the artwork and furniture. But nothing I brought with me is more valuable that what I learned about paying attention to sabaay. I became not only a better contract negotiator but, more important, a better parent, a better teacher, a better friend.

If we all take sabaay into account in our words and interactions with others, we will surely create a more open space for connection and genuine communication.

Embrace the Tiger

Today is my birthday and I feel, well, cranky. Irritable, out of sorts, agitated, restless, not comfortable in my skin. This is puzzling to me since I generally love my birthday. I have no qualms about getting older. In fact, my life just gets better and better, and there is no age I would want to go back to. So why I woke up grumpy on one of my favorite days, I don't know. But the storm clouds ominously gathered—and broke over people who didn't deserve the deluge.

I was waiting for a call from the electrician and asked my daughter to listen for the phone while I took a quick shower. When she told me why she couldn't, I went on a five-minute rant, longer than it would have taken me to shower. After my rant, I still wasn't showered, and I was still upset.

Wow, I thought, *what is going on here?!* I stumbled off to take my shower and started belly breathing to calm down.

Later, I got retroactively testy with a couple of folks who had made mistakes a couple of days ago; then I had taken the mistakes in stride, but today they seemed worthy of detailed comment and not-so-subtle criticism.

I also did a lot of swearing under my breath, in between those belly breaths.

This is where we practice, isn't it? When we are at the edge of what we can handle. When our equanimity is disrupted. When we are hooked by the drama of our own making. When what we want is relief, escape, distraction, a scapegoat. When we want things to be something other than what they are. When we want to be someone other than who we are. The way I feel today. The perfect opportunity to learn.

Charlotte Joko Beck, in *Everyday Zen*, talked about the fragmentation that results when we separate ourselves from our experience. I feel agitated because I am identifying a problem over there, separate from myself, a problem that I want to fix by fixing circumstances or people. If I can fix it, I'll feel better. Everything will be all right. I'll be all right.

This fragmentation triggers fear. The only way I'm really going to feel all right is to return to my natural state of wholeness. How do I do that? By doing what seems counterintuitive. My instincts seek distance and escape from what frightens me. But I've learned that the way back is the way through.

Beck used the image of embracing the tiger. By leaning into my agitation and anger, my fear, rather than trying to fix it or get away from it, I can loosen its grip. She suggests focusing on what is happening in my body. My stomach is tense, I can feel my heart beating faster, my face is scowling, my throat is tight, my head aches, and my mood swings from wanting to yell to wanting to cry.

Oddly, when I do this, when I drop everything else and turn my attention to my nonverbal experience of body sensations right now in this moment, what Beck called walking on the razor's edge, I find what I was really looking for all along: relief. The belly breathing becomes less forced, the tightness releases, my face relaxes, my mind clears like storm clouds parting after the rain.

The calm is fragile. Lightning still flashes on the horizon. I keep coming back, back to now.

I don't know why I'm so "gritchy" today. It will pass if I let it, if I don't hold on to it or struggle against it. I feel better already. The tiger purrs.

> *Tyger! Tyger! burning bright*
> *In the forests of the night*
> —WILLIAM BLAKE

Seasonal Yin Yang

Yesterday was the first day of winter in the northern hemisphere. It was also winter solstice. Interesting that the beginning of winter also marks the beginning of longer daylight. As we enter the time of dark and frozen quiet, the days begin to lengthen, so gradually that most of us don't notice until the morning when we wake up and see the dawn.

Winter solstice is also the middle of the Christmas holiday season. I have been touched by many blog posts during the holiday season about the grief of Christmas instead of the joy. For many people, the holidays mark experiences and anniversaries of loss, betrayal, loneliness, poverty, stress, and despair. My heart breaks open in witness to so much pain.

And yet, within the pain is promise. A friend once said that winter is when the earth is pregnant. What appears to be dead is quietly preparing to burst forth with life. As Bambi's mother assured him, winter does not last forever.

I thought about the yin-yang symbol, the circle with the two curving shapes, one white, one black, in perfect balance and harmony. In the fullest part of the black shape is a small white circle, and in the fullest part of the white shape is a small black circle. Both small circles remind us that the seed for each shape is contained in the other.

Like the seasons. The seed of summer appears in the very beginning of winter as the light lingers longer in the cold, cold days. Likewise, the seed of winter is planted on the first day of summer as the light begins to softly fade, unnoticed as we enjoy walks in the park and iced tea on the porch.

Like summer and winter, joy and sadness come in their seasons. Within each is the seed of the other. We can no more stop their cycle than we can hold on to summer and keep winter at bay. Yet we try. And thereby cause ourselves so much suffering.

As one who was a big believer in the emotional version of daylight savings time, I tried so hard to hold on to the heels of the happy times, bargaining and pleading for just a little longer. The times of sadness were not even acknowledged but instead denied, ignored, swept under rugs of fantasy.

It didn't work. I got tired and gave up. Now the seasons come and go, each one bearing its own precious gifts, each one welcomed in its turn.

> *For everything there is a season, and a time*
> *for every purpose under heaven.*
> –ECCLESIASTES 3:1

The Joy of Sadness, the Sadness of Joy

I sat in the subdued lighting of the ultrasound room. The technician glided the wand over my daughter's growing belly. Too soon, too soon. Too young to be a mother. And yet, there was that blurry blob. Checking, checking. Heart, brain, spine, abdomen, arms and legs, fingers and toes. Everything was there. Surreal.

And finally, the announcement we had been waiting for:

"It's a boy."

With that, the fuzzy little ET-looking thing on the screen became a baby. My grandchild. I started crying. Laughing and crying. Was I sad or happy? I have no idea. All I know was that my heart was full and overflowing.

How am I supposed to make sense of this? My mind tells me stories, stories of judgment and fear, embarrassment and worry. Oh, but my heart. My heart tells me stories of love and forgiveness, acceptance and anticipation, willingness and wonder, trust and faith.

Chögyam Trungpa Rinpoche teaches that joy comes from the gentle heart of sadness. If we can find the courage to stay, to yield, we can sink into the softness of our tender, open heart. With our heart thus exposed and vulnerable, we are connected to the deep heart of all hearts. There we find freedom.

The heart that breaks open can contain the whole universe.
–Joanna Macy

Step 5

Make Haste to Be Kind

Life is short, and we have but little time to gladden the hearts of those who travel this way with us. Oh, be swift to love. Make haste to be kind.
—Henri-Frédéric Amiel

Kindness is one of my favorite steps. First, it's an easy habit to develop, as you will see. And second, you get immediate benefits. For some, like me, it is a welcome relief after the challenges of Steps 3 and 4.

So relax and have some fun. Remember, fun is good!

Heart Hospitality

I like welcome mats. When you walk up to someone's door, the mat tells you something about the people who live there. Is it a functional mat or a fancy one? Perhaps it has a sports logo or birds or flowers on it, or a funny message from the dog or cat. It might say, *No one is a stranger here*, or *Come back with a warrant*.

Hospitality—so many stories and customs. We've heard about families who always have an extra seat at the table for someone stopping by, or extra food to be handed out the back door to the hungry. We've heard about the legendary hospitality of the Bedouins. And Southern hospitality. And the story of the loaves and fishes in the Bible.

And of course my daughter, who used to stand on the front porch when she was little and call out to people passing by—"Hello! Where are you going? Where do you live? Do you have any kids? What's your name?"—until I could race outside and scoop her up.

What about our heart hospitality? Is there room at the table in our soul for one more? Do we turn away strangers?

A Course in Miracles teaches that when we separate ourselves from others not only through actions but even by our thoughts, then we separate ourselves from God. Thoughts of anger, resentment, criticism, envy, fear block our ability to see the divine in everyone.

We have busy lives and good reason to exercise caution for our safety but, in our hearts, can we put the welcome mat out? Can we inwardly greet each person with a sincere invitation to come in from the cold and bask in the warm glow of loving acceptance that embraces us all?

I just went to my front door and looked at the welcome mat. It's dirty and faded and frayed. I'm going to toss it in the trash and go buy a new one.

> *Do not neglect to show hospitality to strangers,*
> *for thereby some have entertained angels unawares.*
> –Hebrews 13:2

That Man Might Be Jesus!

I too often find myself overlooking people in various ways. Not because I'm mean, but because I'm distracted or in a hurry, or because I think I know better. Just the other day I went out to dinner with my son James and caught myself trying to correct his order (for not one but two hamburgers). James is twenty-five years old. He gets to make his own meal decisions.

I was reminded of a story I heard about another boy—an actual child, not an adult, though that still doesn't matter in this context—who went to a restaurant with his parents. When the server asked him what he wanted, he ordered a hot dog and a soda. His mother quickly said, "Oh, no, he'll have the skinless chicken breast with vegetables." His dad added, "And milk instead of soda." The boy looked crestfallen. The server paused and then turned to the boy. "Would you like relish on your hot dog?" she asked. After she left the table, the boy was beaming. "Did you see that?" he exclaimed. "She thinks I'm real!"

An even more startling, poignant example of this happened when I was walking my dog recently in our neighborhood, and a woman working in her yard stopped me to admire Sadie. As she was bent over rubbing Sadie's ears and talking doggie talk to her, a homeless man walked by pushing his rickety grocery cart piled full. The woman jerked up suddenly and bolted for her door, calling back over her shoulder to me, "That man might be Jesus! I have to go fix him a sandwich!"

I was dumbfounded. I waited a moment for the candid camera folks to leap out of the bushes. Then I moved off in the opposite direction, marveling at the bizarre kookiness of people. But before I turned the corner, I paused and looked back at the hunched shoulders of the man shuffling off down the street, oblivious to the commotion his passing had provoked.

I guess the joke was on me after all, because I have never looked at people the same way since. Or maybe I should say I have never *over*looked people the same way since. Everybody became real to me that day, imbued with divine identity. I notice people—in the grocery store, in other cars, on the street, in the news. They all have lives. Just like me. They want the same things I want: to be happy and free from suffering. I'm quicker to smile, to nod a greeting, to send a silent blessing.

Maybe that woman was Jesus. Maybe we all are.

Truly, I say to you, as you did it to one of the least of these,
my brothers, you did it to me.
–Matthew 25:40

What Are You Writing in Your Book?

A young man walks into a church just before the pastor starts the sermon. He doesn't look like everyone else in the congregation. He is different. Very different. His difference makes people in the congregation uncomfortable. He walks down the aisle looking for a seat, but no one scoots over to make room. He continues down the aisle toward the front of the church. The pastor pauses, unsure whether to begin. No one acknowledges the visitor. The tension mounts. When he gets near the front and sees that there is no seat available for him, he quietly sits down on the floor. An elderly deacon walks slowly down the aisle toward him. Everyone is expecting that the deacon will ask him to leave, and they are hoping this unpleasantness will all be over soon. The tension thrums. When the deacon reaches the young man, he awkwardly and with great difficulty lowers himself to the floor to sit next to the visitor and worship alongside him. The pastor says, "What I'm about to preach, you might never remember. What you have just seen, you will never forget."

I was reading a friend's blog recently. She wrote about being called to the phone years ago, when she was in graduate school, because her mother was dying. That call would be the last tender and loving conversation they had. Later that day, someone she didn't know very well said that she had inadvertently overheard the conversation and offered words of comfort as best she could. My friend wrote that these words meant a lot to her and reminded her of the importance of sharing our hearts with everyone.

The writing was so eloquent and deeply moving that I went to my friend and started crying as I expressed my gratitude for her sharing this story. She replied, "Don't you remember? The person who came up to me was you."

In the years since, we have developed a friendship I treasure, but I do not remember this early encounter. I wonder how many other encounters I've forgotten that made some lasting impression on someone else. And what kind of impression did I leave? Some I would not be proud of now, I'm sure.

So my friend gave me two gifts that day. First, the touching story of saying good-bye to her mother. And second, the reminder that with every word and deed, I am writing the book of my life, and I never know when someone will be reading.

Be careful how you live. You might be the only Bible some people will ever read.
—UNKNOWN

The Kindness Game

When my daughter was in high school, she was, like many high school kids, focused on herself. I thought it might do her some good to think outside of her own life. So I came up with a game. Each day we would compete to see who could do the most nice things for other people. It could be something as simple as smiling at someone as you pass by or saying something encouraging. If you did something nice for someone in your family, you got double points, because we often overlook those closest to us. At the end of the day we would compare notes and see who won.

Playing the game was fun. You go through your day a little differently when you are actively seeking opportunities to be kind. I caught myself smiling more, greeting people, listening more attentively, offering to help a little more quickly, finding something nice to say. I wrote out a compliment card for someone who helped me at the store. Mia ate lunch with a student from another country who was often isolated.

One day, Mia called me as she walked home from school and asked me for directions to a certain address. When she got home much later than usual, she explained that she had seen a young woman looking distressed. Mia crossed the street to ask if she needed help. The young woman was developmentally disabled and had gotten off at the wrong bus stop on her way home. She was disoriented and couldn't figure out how to get home. After I gave Mia directions over the phone, she walked the young woman all the way home, even though it was quite a bit out of her way. When she told me the story, I readily conceded the game for that day, for the whole week. I could see that Mia felt compassion for this young woman and was pleased to be able to help her. (Because Mia's brothers have autism, this kindness on Mia's part was especially meaningful. I would like to believe that someone would do the same for them if they were lost.)

Playing the kindness game helps us develop the habit of kindness. The point isn't to "win" or to brag about what a nice person you are. After all, kindness done in secret is often the most delicious. The point of sharing is to help others be more aware of all the opportunities we have as we go through our day to brighten someone's life, to lift someone's spirit. By sharing our examples, we can inspire each other to see those chances we might otherwise overlook.

What a wonderful way to have fun.

> *Three things in human life are important: the first is to be kind; the second is to be kind; and the third is to be kind.*
> –HENRY JAMES

Kindness Pays

When Mia was in middle school, Grace joined the family as a foster daughter and sister. Grace got along with the boys, but she and Mia enjoyed only a brief honeymoon period before the fur started flying. Over time, their animosity became so entrenched that their attacks were automatic. They seemed incapable of seeing, let alone respecting, the other person's perspective. Each saw herself as the victim of the other, on the receiving end of unwarranted meanness, each self-righteous in retaliation.

I did everything I knew to do. We processed ourselves silly, went to counseling, discussed to exhaustion. Consequences were shrugged off.

Finally, I felt forced to keep them separated as much as possible, knowing that if they entered the same space, it would only be seconds before the air ignited with hostility. Getting them to really understand the situation was a futile endeavor. Each was dug in too deeply. I decided I didn't really care anymore if they "got it." I needed the behavior to change, regardless of their understanding.

I made a proposal based on the only thing I thought might motivate them: money. I promised to pay each of them $1 a day to get along. They had to be affirmatively nice to each other—ignoring each other was not enough. Only I got to decide at the end of the day if they earned the money. And either they both earned it or neither did. They would make money or not as a team. Grace observed that this idea might cost me a lot of money. I thought to myself it would be a bargain at twice the price.

It was a bargain indeed. The next day was a pleasure. They said please and thank you to each other. They offered to help each other with chores. They complimented each other. They were totally insincere, you understand. I didn't care. Peace was restored.

By the time the novelty wore off after a few weeks, they had broken their negative habit. And they changed at a deeper level. Breaking the cycle gave them room to breathe. Their defenses relaxed. Being kind, even if it was to get money, felt good. It felt good to the person being kind, and it felt good to the recipient of the kindness. They began to form new behavior habits. And after a while, I didn't need to pay them anymore.

Today Mia and Grace are good friends, even sisters. They laugh at all the things they said and did to each other. (I'm a little slower in seeing the humor.) They apologize and forgive. The wisdom of the slogan "Fake it till you make it" is proven again. Fake kindness leads to genuine kindness. And genuine kindness leads to our happy place.

Small acts of kindness may or may not change the world,
but they definitely change you.
—NIPUN MEHTA

Make Someone's Day!

During a meeting that was getting more tedious by the moment, the woman sitting next to me turned to me and whispered, "You have the nicest smile. I bet everyone tells you that."

Well, no, no one tells me that. My mom probably told me that when I was little; I don't remember. But when this woman told me that, I... Well, I'm embarrassed to admit how pleased I was. I basked in that compliment all day. I smiled at myself in the rearview mirror at traffic lights. I smiled at my children. I smiled at strangers. I just smiled for no reason.

That simple compliment made my day. I woke up the next morning still thinking about it. How easy it is to brighten someone's day with a few kind words. I resolved to look for opportunities to pay her kindness forward.

Not long after that, I took my three-month-old grandson to the grocery store. He was not happy in the cart, so I ended up carrying him in one arm. No problem till I got to the bulk foods and needed two hands to scoop the food I wanted from the bin. I went to the customer service desk and asked for help. A lovely young woman named Emily went with me right away and helped me get what I needed.

Then, when I was checking out, she noticed me in the line and came over to bag my groceries and insisted on carrying them out to the car. When I tried to thank her, she brushed it off, saying she was happy to be outside. She was so gracious and kind.

When I got home, I called the store and told the manager about her exceptional help. The manager was so pleased and assured me that Emily would get some extra recognition. The manager went on to thank me for calling and said that a $5 gift card would be waiting for me at the counter on my next visit. Wow, I didn't see that coming.

I read recently that a 4:1 rule applies to successful relationships. For every negative interaction, there should be four positive ones. I got to thinking that the same ratio could apply to all our interactions. If we complain about something, we could balance that with four positive statements. We could balance every criticism with four compliments. Every expression of irritation or anger could be outweighed with four expressions of love and appreciation.

I had an opportunity to put this into practice once after I had lashed out at someone I thought had messed up. Whether or not the criticism was warranted, the fact was that I didn't feel good about how I expressed it. My frustration was not relieved.

After realizing this, I called the person I had criticized so harshly. I apologized for how I had handled my frustration. I explained more objectively what I thought needed correction, and I put that in the context of the overall great job I thought this person did. I made sure to identify several specific situations when she had done a superb job. We ended that conversation on a much more positive note, and I felt better. I hope she did, too.

Our attacks are rarely about the outside circumstances. They are about us. If we are mindful of the times when we send out negative thoughts and words, we can counter with sending out positive thoughts and words four times as often. Inner harmony will be restored, and we will be a lot happier.

Of course, we don't have to wait for a negative expression to trigger the positive ones. We can build up a reservoir of good energy by looking for opportunities to think or say something good.

The woman who complimented my smile went on with her day and didn't give it another thought, but she made my day with her simple kindness.

> *Kind words are short and easy to speak,*
> *but their echoes are truly endless.*
> –MOTHER TERESA

Speaking the Blessing

Just a little while ago, I turned on the TV while I was putting clean sheets on my bed. (Now that makes my bed a happy place!) I happened to surf across a preacher, Joel Osteen, just as he said something about "speaking the blessing." I am a bit embarrassed to admit that I listened to a televangelist, but the words caught my attention and I paused on the station to hear what he had to say.

He was talking about the power of our words to bless and bestow favor, especially when we speak to those over whom we have authority or influence: our children, our spouses, our students, our employees.

It reminded me of something I wrote to my five children, all adopted or foster, several years ago in a Mother's Day letter:

God has blessed me beyond heaven by entrusting the five of you to my care. All of us have come to this family from other families. This is a family God made. We are together because He brought us together to love one another. As He has blessed me, I bless all of you. Thank you for the honor of being your mother.

I would like to say that this is how I speak to my children all the time. But it isn't. I too often speak to criticize, to demand, to nag. Especially to nag.

I also thought about my students. I taught students at the beginning of their graduate education, when many are insecure. I have heard through others that my students appreciated the way I encouraged them and made them believe they could be successful.

I'm glad I did that. But I wonder if my own kids would say the same thing. I often praise them when I speak to others, and I frequently thank God for them, but do I speak the blessings directly to them? I hope the words I heard on television, as I casually made the bed, will make me more mindful of opportunities to voice my love and pride and confidence in them.

The whole creation responds to praise, and is glad.
–CHARLES FILLMORE

Speak Wisely

Life and death are in the power of our tongue.
—Proverbs 18:21

My daughter Lily and her friend Jamie grew up together in an orphanage in China and were both adopted as teens. Jamie's mom and I took the girls to a mall not long after they had moved to the States. We adults decided to relax in the food court while the girls went shopping. Jamie smiled and admonished us to "speak wisely" before running off to join Lily. I have no idea what she thought we were going to say, or if that was just some quirk in her new language, but I cherish this phrase and the memory of her delivery of it.

"Speak wisely" reminds me of Buddhism's Noble Eightfold Path, which includes Right Speech. It teaches us to ask three questions before we speak. (1) Is it true? (2) Is it necessary? (3) Is it kind? If we can answer all three questions yes, then we are assured that we are speaking wisely.

I don't always speak wisely. I used to love gossip. I am a Southern girl, after all. It's in my blood. Gossip is a way to connect to others, to fit in, to belong, to be popular. When I lived in Paris, I was the only American in my building. I would often practice my French by chatting about the other tenants with the concierge, who spoke no English. I became a bilingual gossiper. And even though she was not too keen on Americans, she liked me. So much so that when I moved out, she gave me the nicest compliment she could think of. "You're not really *very* American," she nodded with approval.

Gossip often seems fun and harmless, but we all know it has a dark side. Gossip can ruin lives, cost people their jobs, drive teens to suicide, destroy friendships and, at the very least, hurt people's feelings. Even if it meets the first criteria and is true, it is rarely necessary or kind.

Gretchen Rubin in *The Happiness Project* cautions against gossip. The thrill of sharing gossip is short-lived. We have to promise and exact promises from others not to tell. We don't really feel good about what we did. We're anxious that the story will get out and be traced back to us. We might feel guilty that we betrayed a confidence or that we spoke ill of someone just to have a moment's pleasure.

I have reformed. As a person who appreciates the power of words, I value Jamie's advice to speak wisely. I honor the trust of someone who shares private information with me. I try to change the topic or excuse myself from gossipy conversations. I don't justify gossip by thinking that I'm not saying anything I wouldn't say directly to the person. If it is something I would say directly to the person, then that is the only place I should say it.

And I try to remember to ask myself, *Is what I'm about to say an improvement on silence?*

If you can't say somethin' nice, don't say nothin' at all.
—THUMPER, IN *BAMBI*

It's Not About You

All the joy the world contains has come through wishing happiness for others. All the misery the world contains has come through wanting pleasure for oneself.
—Shantideva

As a law professor, I had a standard speech for first-year students:

> Your professional responsibility doesn't begin when you pass the bar exam. It begins today. The people who will be coming to you for help are depending on your expertise, your integrity, and your effort. Your education up till now has been about you, but beginning today, it isn't about you anymore. It's about them.

In spite of this hopefully motivating wisdom I imparted to my students, I have often lived my own life as if it is all about me. Those are not my happiest times.

Once, I was going through an especially trying time, feeling burdened and unfairly treated. And whiny, very whiny. After a while, I was even more unhappy about being so chronically disgruntled. I saw an announcement about a volunteer opportunity as a trained spiritual companion. Not a therapist or a minister but a person trained to "walk beside" a person who was having difficulty. I signed up. I learned that the care relationship was not about me but about the person needing my attention. I learned to put myself aside and listen to someone else. Really listen. After the training was complete, I had care receivers. The time I spent helping someone else was time I was not spending thinking about my own problems. What a relief! Amazingly, the more I helped other people, the smaller my own problems became. I was happier both because I wasn't wallowing in self-pity and because I was being of service to others.

As much as we need a prosperous economy, we also need
a prosperity of kindness and decency.
–CAROLINE KENNEDY

A Few Leaves

No act of kindness, however small, is wasted.

—Aesop

As I was driving to visit my sons one fall day, I noticed a woman in a wheelchair on the sidewalk next to a van parked at the curb. The van had a side ramp that was partially unfolded, but seemed to be stuck. The woman held something in her hand—I couldn't tell if it was a control for the van or perhaps a cell phone. As I passed by, I looked for a driver or someone nearby who might be helping her, but I saw no one.

I continued another block or two, wondering whether an offer of help would be an unwelcome intrusion, and also thinking of the time, since I was already late to visit my sons. Nevertheless, I circled back to see if she was still there. Sure enough, nothing had changed. I pulled over behind her van, got out, and asked her if she needed some help. Yes, she said. If I could just pull on the bottom section of the ramp, it would flatten out. It was easy enough to do, requiring only a gentle tug. The ramp had gotten stuck on a small pile of autumn leaves. I asked her if she needed further assistance to get in the van or to get the ramp back up, but she assured me she could do the rest herself.

It took me all of forty-five seconds to hop out of my car, unstick her ramp, get back into my car, and drive off. But I spent the next several hours thinking about this brief encounter.

This woman had a state-of-the-art wheelchair and van so that she could move about independently. A marvel of technology and engineering, providing self-sufficiency and freedom. Yet she was immobilized by a few leaves that I would never have even noticed had I been heading for my car. The event made me realize how blessed I am that I have legs that can walk.

Even more than that, it reminded how easy it is for me to help someone. A few seconds of my time solved that woman's problem and allowed her to continue with her day.

> *Never tell your neighbor to wait till tomorrow*
> *if you can help them now.*
> –PROVERBS 3:28

Put Your Oxygen Mask on First

Those of us who fly often can recite the flight attendant's instructions in our sleep:

> In the unlikely event of a loss of cabin pressure, a mask will drop down from your over-head compartment. Secure the mask around your head and breathe normally. If you are traveling with a child or someone who needs assistance, secure your own oxygen mask first, and then offer assistance to your companion.

When we first heard these instructions, we might have thought that in such a crisis we would help our loved ones first. However, on further reflection, we understood that we could help our loved ones better if we weren't passing out from lack of oxygen ourselves!

When we start talking about kindness, we often overlook ourselves. Some of us think we should give and give until we are depleted. To focus kindness on ourselves seems wrong. But this is not selfish. It's not a me-only attitude. It is a wise recognition that being gentle with ourselves is the model for how we treat others.

Although there are many contexts in which we might fail to be kind to ourselves, parenting is a big one. My best model for being a good parent was a dog! When my dog had puppies, seven of them, I spent hours watching her and her squirmy little bundles of joy. The puppies would all sleep in a big heap. When one woke up, they all woke up and started yelping for food. Mama dog would sniff them all to be sure they were fine, and then she turned her back on her frantic pups and calmly walked over to her food dish. She would eat her fill, occasionally lifting her head and cocking her ears toward the corner where her puppies were rooting around for her. After a drink of water, she would go through the dog door to the back yard to relieve herself. Only then did she return to her pups, ready now to tend to their needs, which she did lovingly and thoroughly.

It was still years before I became a mom myself, but I knew at the time I was watching something I should pay attention to. *File this away*, I thought, *and remember to take care of myself so that I can take care of my children.*

And in many ways I did. I took lots of bubble baths. I did not feel bad about leaving my kids with trusted childcare providers so that I could have dinner with a friend, or have some time by myself at the cabin, or take an occasional short vacation.

When the energetic oxygen in our home was depleted, I put my mask on first. Not only was I a much better mom, but my kids saw me taking care of myself. Now that two of them are moms themselves, I see that they are doing a great job of eating right and grabbing sleep when they can.

> *Friendship with oneself is all important, because without it one cannot be friends with anyone else in the world.*
> —ELEANOR ROOSEVELT

Mi Casa Es Su Casa

Hospitality is making your guests feel at home,
even though you wish they were.
–Unknown

When I was a young hippie wannabe, I hitchhiked with a friend through Mexico and Central America to South America, where we planned to spend the winter before heading to Alaska to work on the salmon fishing boats. Along the way, we stayed in modest (read: dirt cheap) accommodations, sometimes a home that rented rooms. These homes were often in the shape of a square, with all the rooms opening onto a small, central courtyard.

I remember one place in particular. It was a hot afternoon in southern Mexico, and I decided to spend it reading in the home's interior courtyard. I soon noticed a child staring at me. I tried out some high school Spanish, and soon we were pointing at things and naming them in Spanish and English. A little later, some people who appeared to be the child's family joined us, offering one of their cool beverages to me. I stayed on for a while, pleased to be mingling with the locals.

Let me make sure you have an accurate picture here. I was, at least at that moment, an unwashed, immodestly dressed, in-full-bloom flower child, hanging with this rather elegant, proper Mexican family, who did their best to make me feel welcome as they passed the heat of the day in this pleasant corner of the hacienda, while I pestered them with my tedious attempts to communicate.

Later that evening, one of the other guests, a more experienced traveler than I, took me aside and told me that I had been sitting with the owners of the home on their private patio. That trip was long ago and I have many memories of it, but none that taught me as much as that family, who, instead of shooing me away so that they could enjoy their afternoon siesta, graciously treated me as an honored guest.

Memories of kindness can bring that past pleasure into our present. And sharing these memories can increase our own happiness and the happiness of the listener. When I invited members of my monthly discussion group on the 10 Steps to share kindness memories, it was interesting that many of us remembered things from childhood.

I remembered Mr. and Mrs. Lubrani, our elderly next-door neighbors who had no kids. Mr. Lubrani maintained a compost pile, uncommon in those days. In the fall, he would rake leaves not only from his own yard but from other yards as well. He let me hang out with him. I helped him with the physical labor, and he taught me about the science of composting. I remember digging my hand into the middle of the pile and feeling the heat generated by the decaying leaves as he explained it to me.

At the end of our work, Mrs. Lubrani would call us in for tea and cookies. I don't remember what we talked about as we sat together on the couch, but I remember feeling good about my time with her. I felt calm and happy. I remember how interested she was in whatever I had to say.

All these decades later, the Lubranis' kindness still warms my heart.

New Best Friend

I have tried to raise kids who are kind. Have I been successful? My answer depends on what day you ask me. But a recent conversation with another parent reminded me of one time when I thought I had lost the battle.

One afternoon when my daughter Mia was in first grade, her teacher called me to tell me that she had been part of a group of children who were cruelly teasing a classmate about his severe allergies and the accommodations that were necessary to keep him safe. I couldn't believe that *my* child would act like that.

I sat Mia in her timeout chair and stood over her, my finger jabbing the air in front of her little chest. I ranted about our family values and that kindness was at the top of the list. I tell you this part of the story to acknowledge that this was not my kindest moment as a parent!

Then I laid out her consequences: "Peter is now your new best friend. If anyone teases him, you will defend him. For the next two weeks, you will sit in this chair for five minutes every morning before you go to school, and you will plan three nice things to do for him that day. Then you will come home after school and tell me about doing them. Furthermore, every night you will sit in this chair for five minutes and make a list of ways to be a good friend, not just to Peter but to everyone."

Amazingly, she did as told and, even more amazingly, became the boy's genuine best friend. She felt good about being kind and by the end of the two weeks was looking forward to planning her nice gestures. It was a great way to start her day.

Deliberately seek opportunities
for kindness, sympathy, and patience.
—EVELYN UNDERHILL

Fake-It-Till-You-Make-It Kindness

Sometimes, we don't feel kind. We don't even want to feel kind. It's possible that this is the best time to *be* kind. Kindness is a great thing because we don't always have to feel it to get the benefit of it. A kind act can generate a subsequent feeling of kindness.

I had a supervisor years ago who was, as the saying goes, a child of God cleverly disguised as a total jerk. He made all our lives miserable. His method of management was to criticize and humiliate. I dreaded having to talk to him. One day I just decided to be outwardly nice. I wasn't making a strategic or an enlightened decision. I just did it. I thanked him for helping me with a project, even though his "help" was to tell me I was doing it all wrong. I asked his opinion on another matter. That threw him off balance so much he actually gave me a compliment!

I would like to tell you that our department was transformed into one big happy family, but it wasn't. What did change was my attitude. I no longer saw myself as a victim. I went about my business and wasn't so churned up. I began to see why he might act the way he did, and even felt compassion for him. The kindness became genuine. No, we were never buddies, but we developed a more positive working relationship.

I'm not suggesting that we use kindness as a way to manipulate someone, or that we use kindness when we are in danger, or that we use it as an assault of our own (as in, "Take that!"). What I am sug-gesting is that sometimes a kind gesture can break through our own feelings of judgment or defensiveness and soften our own hearts. And that can lead to a feeling of well-being and a capacity for genu-ine kindness.

> *Do something wonderful for someone else today,*
> *and you will make two people happy.*
> –UNKNOWN

The Kindness of Strangers

For I was hungry and you gave me food,
I was thirsty and you gave me drink,
I was a stranger and you welcomed me.
–MATTHEW 25:35

I once read a news story about a passerby who pulled an accident victim from a burning car. I have watched a video of a group of people who ran to the aid of a motorcyclist who had been hit by a car and was trapped underneath. The car was on fire. The people actually lifted the car up enough for someone to pull him out from under the car and to safety before the car exploded.

I was in a bad car accident once. I was driving on a two-lane highway in Arkansas at night. As I approached a curve on the outside, a pickup truck driving too fast in the other direction swung wide into my lane. I veered, lost control in the gravel, and plunged off the road. My car flipped down an embankment and ended up upside down. I was on the roof of the car in the dark, disoriented and in shock. I was most concerned for my two dogs. I found them in the rear of the car and managed to climb out one of the doors with them and scramble through the brush back up to the road.

By that time, several cars had stopped and people were starting down the embankment to help me. I felt a twinge in my shoulder, and when I reached to touch it realized that my collarbone was smashed.

There was some discussion among my rescuers. One young couple was headed in the direction of the nearest hospital. They loaded me and the dogs in their car and off we went. At the hospital, they came in with me. Once they saw I was in good hands, they took my dogs home with them. When friends were able to pick me up hours later, the two strangers brought my dogs back to the hospital. (They must have given their phone number to someone at the hospital.) In my shock, and by that time drugged state, I didn't even get their names.

At some point in our lives, we all find ourselves, as Blanche so famously said in *A Streetcar Named Desire*, dependent on the kindness of strangers. Sometimes, we are that stranger offering kindness to someone else. And in those moments, whether giving or receiving help, we realize what at other times we so easily forget.

There are no strangers.

> *My religion is kindness.*
> –THE DALAI LAMA

Step 6

Judge Not

We don't see things as they are. We see them as we are.
–ANAÏS NIN

So here we will begin to disentangle ourselves from our habit of judging and begin to develop a habit of keeping our minds and hearts open.

Judging can take many forms, some obvious, some subtle. But all forms have the same effect. Judging always leads to separation. And separation always leads us away from happiness.

Here Comes the Judge

Judge not, that you be not judged.
For with the judgment you pronounce you will be judged.
–MATTHEW 7:1-2

I've always found that verse sobering. Definitely not very cheery. As a retired lawyer, I have visions of the judge sitting behind the bench, glaring down at the hapless miscreant.

When I was five, I got my first diary. I ran across it a while back when I was cleaning out the attic. My first diary entries went something like this.

January 1—Carolyn is good.
January 2—David is good.
January 3—Donny is not good.
January 4—Mary is good.
January 5—Becky is not good.

Wow. I must not have been reading my Bible! I was not at all squeamish about pronouncing definitive judgment. No shades of gray. Next time a five-year-old gives you an appraising glance, be very afraid.

A *Course in Miracles* teaches that any separation from any other person is a separation from God. How do we separate ourselves from people? By judging, criticizing, hating, fearing, labeling, dismissing, stereotyping, condemning. By seeing them as "other."

Ponder that for a moment. Every time you separate yourself from another person with a judging thought, word, or action, you are separating yourself from God. Every time.

On the other hand, it is very hard not to see as separate that person who was really rude in the checkout line at the grocery store. Or the homeless person reeking of booze asking us for money. Or the CEO of a bailed-out company pocketing a gazillion-dollar bonus. Or the ex.

Yet many faiths and psychological theories stand firm on the foundation that our ticket to our happy place is our connection with others. Which brings us to the good news. Every time we open our hearts and connect with another person, we connect to God. Every time.

> *When you see a good person,*
> *think about evaluating that person.*
> *When you see a bad person,*
> *think about evaluating yourself.*
> —CONFUCIUS

Spinning Straw into Gold

Just as the miller's daughter in Rumpelstiltskin was called upon to spin straw into gold, so we have been given the opportunity to turn a judging thought into a kind thought. I took a beach vacation one summer. I confess I often reacted to the thousands of people in bathing suits with less than charitable thoughts.

You should not be wearing that bikini, girlfriend.

That Speedo is not doing you any favors, bro.

After a couple of days, I realized that I was poisoning my own spirit with these thoughts. All those folks were soaking up sunshine and having a great time without any regard to my opinion, and rightfully so. I decided that every time I had a judgmental thought, I would turn it into a positive one.

To bikini girl: *That's a great color on you.*

To Speedo guy: *I admire your self-confidence.*

My mood improved so much that I started passing out silent compliments at every opportunity.

Love your accent.

Nice smile.

Great job.

It seemed that everywhere I looked, there was something or someone to send a pleasant thought to. Not only did my thoughts change, but my whole outlook changed, like straw into gold. I found myself humming a familiar tune.

> *You've got to accentuate the positive*
> *Eliminate the negative*
> *And latch on to the affirmative*
> *Don't mess with Mister In-Between.*
> —JOHNNY MERCER

Complaint-Free Challenge

Oh man, I am sick of this rain. I didn't sleep at all last night. I ate too much. What is wrong with my team? I can't believe I have to work late again. That movie was a waste of money.

One of the most common ways we judge is by complaining. Sometimes, I catch myself complaining when someone asks me how I am, or how my week is going. Why do I do that? Like many people, I often complain as a way of connecting with someone. Misery sure loves company. How often do we roll our eyes with another person about the weather, for example? Why do we try to connect with each other by sharing our annoyances rather than by sharing our joys?

Complaining keeps us from our happy place by focusing on negatives. It invites others to join us in this negative place. We can change this habit. Will Bowen started a program called *A Complaint Free World*. Based on studies showing that it takes about twenty-one days of consistent practice to form a new habit, he encouraged his church congregation to replace the habit of complaining with the habit of being positive. Everyone wore a purple plastic bracelet as a visual reminder. Each time a person caught herself complaining, she would switch the bracelet to the other wrist. The goal was to go twenty-one consecutive days without switching that bracelet. I would be happy to go twenty-one minutes!

To change a habit, we must first be aware of it. When do we tend to complain? To whom? About what? How do we feel when we're complaining? How do other people respond?

Once we become aware of our complaint habits, we need to substitute a more desirable habit. If you want a toddler to hand over some inappropriate but coveted object, what is the best approach? Yank it from his hand? Or offer him something more attractive? Our minds work the same way. If we simply try to stop the bad habit, it will flow back in to fill the void. We need to give our brain something better to do. We need to create a new habit.

When we catch ourselves complaining, we can substitute a positive thought or comment. With practice, we will catch ourselves just before we complain, and we can connect with others through positive comments instead. We will feel happier, and we will lift up those around us. Misery might love company, but joy creates company. Good company. Martin Luther King Jr. inspired millions by describing his dream rather than by describing his pain. We can practice by thinking of common complaints and substituting positive comments. For example, instead of complaining about the rain, we could focus on the lush, green vegetation and the rainbow of flowers it produces. Or we can use a generic positive thought like, *Life is good.*

I took the complaint-free challenge a couple of years ago, and I enjoyed the positive effects. I admit I never made it to twenty-one days in a row but, through repeated effort, I did significantly reduce my complaining ways and develop a habit of positive thinking and interaction with others. Now when I catch myself relapsing into my old complaining ways, I am much quicker to see it and to redirect my thinking.

> *Being happy doesn't mean that everything is perfect. It means that you've decided to look beyond imperfections.*
> –T. Bernard

Expecting Ponies

My life has been full of terrible misfortunes,
most of which never happened.
–MONTAIGNE

There were two boys. One was an optimist; the other was a pessimist. The pessimist was left in a room piled high with every toy a boy could ever desire. The optimist was left in a room piled high with horse manure. After a while, the pessimist was found sitting in a corner of the room, the toys untouched. When asked why he wasn't playing with the toys, he replied sullenly, "Why bother? They will just break anyway." The optimist was discovered laughing with glee and digging like crazy in the horse manure. When asked about his strange behavior, he exclaimed without missing a beat, "I know there's a pony in here somewhere!"

Sometimes, I am more like the boy in the room full of toys. Once I was anticipating an event I was to attend. I was not looking forward to it. I was pretty sure I would be bored. I didn't think I would fit in with that particular crowd. I thought about ways I could justify not going, or excuses for leaving early. By late afternoon, I felt a headache coming on, and that added to my conviction that the evening was going to be a major drag.

As you've probably guessed, the evening was a total delight. The event itself was stimulating and enjoyable. The people were friendly and easy to talk to. The time flew, and I came home pleased and excited about new things I had experienced and new connections I had made.

I wasted a lot of time prejudging the event in a negative way, stewing in a bad mood, and fretting, when I could have just as easily chosen to anticipate having a good time and enjoyed my afternoon before the event. Even if the evening had turned out to be less than excellent, I could have chosen to make the best of it and have fun anyway. I could have kept an open mind and perhaps discovered something or someone interesting. At the very least, I could have chosen to be at peace in the present moment.

The optimistic boy did not find a pony in the pile of horse manure. But he had a joyous time looking.

I Have To vs. I Get To

One way of complaining, or judging, is making I-have-to statements. *I have to go to work. I have to cook dinner for the kids. I have to pay bills.* How many times a day do I start a sentence with "I have to"? Lots more than I realize, I bet.

Think of something you "have" to do. How does that make you feel? When I say "I have to," I feel resistance, like I really don't want to do it. I might feel resentful or grumpy or powerless or overwhelmed. I'm not likely to do whatever it is with a good attitude. I'm not likely to feel happy about it.

But what happens if we change one word? What happens if we change "I have to" to "I get to"? How do we feel now?

Instead of having to go to work, I get to go to work. I have a job when so many people are out of work. I get to be around other people whose company I enjoy. I am paid well for work that I can do well.

Instead of having to cook dinner for the kids, I get to cook dinner for the kids. I have kids whom I adore, and who appreciate a good meal. I have access to healthy food grown by people who work hard to provide my family with an amazing variety of delicious things to eat. I have a kitchen full of tools and appliances to help me prepare the food quickly and easily.

Instead of having to pay the bills, I get to pay the bills. I have electricity and water that come right to my home. I can watch my favorite team on cable TV from the comfort of my couch. I can pay for services provided by skilled people who can fix things, paint things, and save me time.

All of a sudden, instead of feeling burdened by all the things I have to do, I feel blessed beyond belief by all the things I get to do. How did I get to be so lucky?

Nothing is good or bad, but thinking makes it so.
                              −SHAKESPEARE

Family Habits

Just as I can settle into habits that lead me away from my happy place, my family as a unit can sometimes do the same. As my kids grew up, there were times it seemed we were in a rut of criticizing and complaining. Here are a few things I tried from time to time to break the cycle.

One daughter got in the habit of coming home from school and immediately launching into a list of things that went wrong during her day. I tried patiently listening and then tuning her out, but it was a downer. She was unaware of her own habit. It was her way of coming home and engaging, but she didn't understand the energy drain of focusing on the negative.

So I tried something different. Before she got started with her first complaint, I would ask her to tell me about something good that happened at school. Sometimes she had a hard time shifting her focus to the positive, but once she could identify one thing, I would ask questions to expand the conversation about that event. That often led to remembering other good things that happened. The recount of good tidings helped make the transition from school to home more pleasant for all. And it helped to identify the occasional distressing event that warranted debriefing.

As a family, we sometimes fell into a pattern of criticism and hurt feelings and misunderstandings. We started a practice of appreciation dinners, especially at times when tensions were high and we were all feeling grumpy with each other. We began dinner by each person identifying something to appreciate about every other person at the table. It might be a quality of that person, or something that person did or said. Sometimes this got pretty funny, especially when it was James's and Dan's turns. Their autism gives them a unique perspective, so what they appreciated was sometimes quite unexpected!

I learned that we feed off of each other in our family, and I suspect other families are like that, too. One person's complaints will trigger another person's. Likewise, one person focusing on something positive will invite others to do the same.

Let us not pass judgment on one another any longer,
but rather decide never to put a stumbling block or hindrance
in the way of a brother.
–ROMANS 14:13

Another's Moccasins

Don't judge someone until you walk a mile in his moccasins.
–NATIVE AMERICAN PROVERB

Have you ever been annoyed in a store or a restaurant or on a plane by a child misbehaving? What was your reaction? We might think that the child is a brat, that the mother is a bad parent, that kids these days are not taught good manners, that the civilized world is going down the toilet.

More times than not, when my son James was growing up, I was the mother with the misbehaving child. He would not look you in the eye. He liked to make animal noises. He had a low tolerance for certain stimuli, such as amplified voices, crowds, being touched. He did not like a change in plans or a disappointed expectation. Of course, many kids and even adults share some of these traits. But for James, something he did not like could cause a total meltdown, with screaming and crying. Once his anxiety began to escalate, it was very difficult to avoid a tantrum, and once triggered, the tantrum wrecked the rest of the day.

Trying to engage in normal activities, like going to the grocery store, often left me drained and in despair. More times than I can remember, as James began to whine and ramp up, I could see eyes darting my way, lips pursing, eyebrows frowning, heads shaking. I wanted to scream, "He's autistic! I'm doing the best I can. I just need to get something for dinner."

Once I took him to McDonald's for a Happy Meal. After he ate, he wanted to play in the plastic-ball pit. He got in and started jumping around. He was having a great time. Then a little girl got in, too. James was ignoring her, but he was making his animal sounds, and the little girl got nervous. Who could blame her? I was trying to coax James back to the entrance to leave, but he was at the far side. The little girl's dad looked quizzically at James and then began to scowl. "Your son should not be in there if you can't control him," he said to me. I went home and cried.

I am not denying that there are bratty kids out there, or bad moms. And I'm not denying that James had his bratty moments, or that I had my bad-mom moments, more than I care to remember. My point is that we don't always know what is going on in someone else's life. Perhaps the mother who appears to be ignoring her misbehaving child is overwhelmed. Perhaps the child has OCD or autism or something else that affects her behavior.

Rushing to judgment blocks our ability to feel and express compassion. When I was in a position to explain what was going on with James, I found people to be universally kind and supportive. Now that James is grown, his disability is immediately apparent, and people are quick to be friendly. When we have information, we often put our best foot forward. When we don't have information, perhaps we still could put that same foot in the other person's moccasin.

If we could read the secret history of our enemies, we should find in each man's life sorrow and suffering enough to disarm all hostility.
–HENRY WADWORTH LONGFELLOW

Joy with the Morning

Weeping may tarry for the night,
but joy comes with the morning.
–PSALM 30:5

I wept a lot when my son was growing up. From the moment I heard the word *autism*, I set out to fix him, to use my love, my intelligence, my resources, my will, my faith to make him well. His continued autism signified failure.

One morning when James was a teenager, I passed the partially open bathroom door as he was brushing his teeth. He was looking in the mirror and making faces and laughing. Then he exclaimed, with such exuberant enthusiasm, "It's *great* to be James!"

Wow. All those years I thought it must be terrible to be James. And all those years he thought being James was terrific.

James didn't need healing. I did. I realized that my suffering wasn't being inflicted on me from "out there." My suffering was self-inflicted, resulting from my own perception of James's life, and my own denial of the impact of his autism on my life. I started questioning my assumptions.

There is a Zen story about a poor, old farmer. One day his only horse ran away. His neighbor said, "How unfortunate that your horse ran away. Now you can't plow your field." The farmer replied,

"Who knows if it is good or bad?" The next day the horse returned, leading twenty wild horses. The neighbor said, "How wonderful! Now you are a rich man." The farmer replied, "Who knows if it is good or bad?" The next day, his only son broke his leg while trying to tame one of the horses. The neighbor said, "What a tragedy. Now your son is crippled." The farmer replied, "Who knows if it is good or bad?" The next day, the army came to the village and drafted all the young men to fight in a war far away. The farmer's son was the only one spared.

We create so much suffering for ourselves with our judgments. We assume that we know what we don't know, what we can't know. Have you ever had your plans thwarted only to realize later that things turned out better than what you had planned? Who was I to say that James's autism was good or bad? Perhaps a mustard seed of faith meant trusting God's divine plan. Perhaps everything is perfect in God's eyes. Perhaps James is perfect.

> *Trust in the Lord with all your heart, and do not lean on your own understanding. In all your ways acknowledge him, and he will make straight your paths.*
>
> –PROVERBS 3:5-6

Mirror, Mirror on the Wall

Why do you see the speck that is in your brother's eye,
but do not notice the log that is in your own eye?
–Matthew 7:3

Sometimes we are our own harshest critics, especially when we are criticizing someone else.

A colleague at the law school sent an e-mail to the registrar complaining about his teaching schedule. Because he thought my schedule was part of the unfairness to him, I was copied on it. In the ensuing series of e-mails, he questioned the "power" of another teacher to be able to claim the coveted time slot.

Not sure if he was joking (I didn't know him very well), I deflected the issue with some weak humor. Afterward, I pondered the exchange, labeled his side as petty ego trip, and privately gifted him with some condescending compassion. I saw myself as quite above such a silly fray. Way too spiritual, too serene, too wise. Concerned more with real suffering in the world than whether I would be coming home an hour later usual from work.

Basking in my moral superiority as I condemned his sense of workplace superiority (you see where this is going), I suddenly "saw" a mirror in front of me. I remembered when an hour in my schedule meant the difference between being able to pick up my kids after school or needing after-school childcare. I didn't know anything about my colleague's personal life. That hour might be very important. Indeed, I remember times when I was practically apoplectic over being kept waiting ten minutes. Who was I to judge this colleague?

Disappointed that my enjoyment of being more-enlightened-than-thou was so abruptly cut short, I started wondering if there was anything I could judge someone for that I wasn't guilty of myself. Surely there was something I could point at and say with confidence, "I never have done and never would do that!" After several hours, I couldn't think of anything that I was not guilty of, either directly or indirectly.

About the same time as the incident with the colleague, I was struggling more deeply with one of my teenage daughter's careless and selfish choices. Her decision changed her life and the lives of those around her, including mine. I was feeling resentful and angry. How could she be so unthinking about the consequences of her actions, so cavalier about their impact on others?

Then I remembered myself at her age. I was every parent's worst nightmare. All I can say is that I must have had a whole platoon of guardian angels on 24/7 duty, because it is truly a miracle that I did not destroy my life and take a few others down with me during my tumultuous adolescence. As I said to one of my other kids when she was amazed that I caught her doing something she was sure she could get away with, "Honey, you are not even in my league." I am so glad my parents lived long enough to see me turn into a halfway decent human being. When I think of my own youth, I fall to my knees in gratitude for every one of my kids.

Seeing our judgments reflected back to us certainly takes the fun out of judging!

> *Everything that irritates us about others can lead us*
> *to an understanding of ourselves.*
> –CARL JUNG

What Do Real Americans Look Like?

During the 2008 election campaign, one candidate referred to the crowd as "real Americans." Who do you think was in the audience? More significantly, who wasn't? What is your image of a real American?

In 2010, the Virginia governor designated April as Confederate History Month. In his proclamation, the governor omitted any reference to slavery, which sparked debate about what Confederate history really means and whether it is something to be proud of or ashamed of.

As a child of the South, this is my history, too. I remember having a discussion with my nephew years ago when he was a young man attending college in Mississippi. He wanted to put a Confederate flag sticker on his car to show school spirit. He had no political intent at all and didn't associate the symbol with its history. He did not appreciate how this symbol could offend people. Even when I explained what the symbol might represent to African Americans, he thought I was making a big deal out of something that was innocent and fun.

We often do that, don't we? We assume that our reality is everyone's reality, and if they see things differently, they must be mistaken.

My daughter, who is Chinese and grew up in China, sometimes uses the term *American* to mean *White*. When she does, I remind her that she is an American. She rolls her eyes and says, "You know what I mean." And I reply, "Yes, and you know what I mean!" My children are all of different races and ethnic backgrounds. Some were born in the United States; others weren't. Their faith cultures of origin are Buddhist, Christian, Muslim. They are all United States citizens. They are real Americans.

> *Give me your tired, your poor, your huddled masses*
> *yearning to breathe free.*
>
> –Emma Lazarus (inscribed on the Statue of Liberty)

Judging Aziza

Assumptions. We all make them. Most of the time we don't even realize it. And most of the time, they do no harm. But sometimes they separate us in quietly insidious ways. That doesn't make us bad. It makes us human. But what happens when we catch ourselves making these assumptions, when we question them, when we consider that the beliefs we hold based on these assumptions are built on shaky ground?

I once had a housemate who was African American. I'm Caucasian. I often read her magazines, many of which were focused on the African American community. I remember a story in *Jet* about an entire family electrocuted while out on a picnic. A power line fell onto the family's car. One person touched the car and each person in turn tried to help by grabbing the people already captured by the current. The entire family died. Later, I related this horrific tragedy to my friend, but didn't think to mention where I had read it or the ethnicity of the family, neither of which seemed relevant to the story.

A few days after that, she came up to me wide-eyed and exclaimed, "You won't believe what happened. That story you told me about the family that got electrocuted? The same thing happened to a Black family!"

"You mean to say," I replied, "that it is easier to believe that the exact same freak accident happened to a White family *and* a Black family, than to consider the possibility that a White woman read a Black-oriented magazine?"

We just stood there looking at each other.

Of course, I make such assumptions, too. When I was still fairly new to blogging, a commenter on my blog mentioned that he was headed off to bed. Since I was enjoying my morning cup of tea, that caught my attention. Here is the exchange that followed.

> Me: Oh, are you a night owl?
> Him: No, I'm in Singapore.
> Me: Are you traveling or working there?
> Him: No, I'm Singaporean Chinese.
> Me: I'm studying Chinese.
> Him: I don't really speak Chinese.
> Me: Wow, you are a one-person lesson in assumptions. Here are the ones I've already made about you. (1) All my readers are in the US so you must be, too. (2) If you are not in the US, you must still be an American. (3) If you are ethnic Chinese, you must speak Chinese. Thank you for this lesson.

Understand that I am a person who has lived and worked and traveled overseas and have many friends who are not American. And I have a Chinese daughter who doesn't speak Chinese. And yet I still jumped to these assumptions.

Well, you might say, those are harmless. Indeed, this commenter and I laughed it off and became close blog friends. But are they harmless? How do my unquestioned assumptions color the way I think about people, about how they act and think, about how they might be safe or not safe, my friends or my enemies? Here is a more telling example.

The first time I saw her, she came to my house along with the young woman who was my regular babysitter. Our babysitter was suggesting this woman as her replacement. When she walked in the door, this is what I saw: Lots of metal on her clothes and through her skin. All-black clothing and boots that looked like lethal weapons. Latte-brown skin and smoldering dark eyes. And then I heard her exotic Arabic name I couldn't pronounce without some practice.

Oh dear, I worried. *I hope she isn't staying. She should not be around children, especially my children. She would not know how to act with children. She's probably not very smart. She probably does drugs. She looks dangerous. Maybe she is armed. My children would be afraid of her. Heck, I'm afraid of her.*

Most of these were not conscious thoughts. But looking back, I'm sure some of those assumptions were lurking beneath the surface.

Fast forward. Aziza became my most trusted and respected child-care provider. She is one of the most caring and intelligent people I've ever met. She has impeccable integrity. She has deep wisdom about children, and I often asked her opinion. My kids adored her. When she picked Mia up after school, Mia's popularity immediately rose because no other kid had a sitter anywhere as cool as Aziza. All the kids crowded around to get a chance to talk to her, to be in her presence. She was the pied piper of middle school.

We still keep in touch. She is a well-known poet and social activist. She will leave her mark on this world, and the world will be better for it. I know she left her mark on my family and we are better for it.

I don't think it's possible to eliminate all our assumptions, but if we can become more aware of them, and more questioning of them, we can begin to see each other without all the filters.

Vision or judgment is your choice, but never both of these.
—*A COURSE IN MIRACLES*

Who Is a Terrorist?

We have met the enemy and he is us.
–POGO

Terrorism is a word we use a lot these days. We are engaged in a war on terror. We identify certain people as terrorists. When you think of the word *terrorist*, what is the first image that comes to mind? The first image, without thinking about it.

What does your terrorist look like? Man or a woman? From what part of the world? Of what faith? Of what race or ethnic group?

Okay, now imagine that you are a Native American living on the plains in the 1800s. You are cooking breakfast early one morning, and you hear horses coming. Soldiers ride through your village killing everyone while other soldiers play music. Would you call them terrorists? What did they look like? Where were they from? Of what faith? Of what race?

Or describe a *revolutionary*. What is the first thing you think of? Is it the revolutionary soldiers we revere today who fought for our independence from England? Were they called heroes in England? Or terrorists?

In her book *Taking the Leap*, Pema Chödrön talked about the word *haji*. Soldiers serving in the Middle East learn to use this word to dismiss or dehumanize civilians, as in, "They're just haji." But in

Islamic culture, the word is an honorific term for one who has made the pilgrimage to Mecca.

Words. Words that we attach different meanings to. Meanings that connect us or separate us.

One time I was walking in the hills outside a charming Bavarian town in Germany. I followed a path through the woods to a small church, peacefully nestled in the trees. The building's exterior walls, protected by colonnades, were covered with old black-and-white photos of soldiers. Young men sent off to war, probably from the nearby town. Loved and honored by their families. Some of them might have killed or been killed by my country's young men sent off to war. Standing there in front of hundreds of pictures, I found it hard to identify the heroes and the villains.

I remember an argument I had years ago with my soon-to-be ex-husband. I wanted the divorce. He didn't. I wanted him to understand my reasons. I wanted him to agree that what I was doing was best for both of us. I desperately wanted him to see that I was not a bad person. We sat in two chairs facing each other and argued for hours. I was exhausted. I'm sure he was, too. Suddenly, I had what I can only describe as an out-of-body experience. I found myself sitting in his chair, looking through his eyes at me. I felt his feelings and thought his thoughts. He felt angry at my stubborn refusal to acknowledge what I was doing. I was breaking his heart. He felt helpless to stop me. His perspective was crystal clear to me and completely understandable. Reality depended on what chair I was sitting in.

It is hard to imagine what the world looks like from the chair of a terrorist. The very label identifies that person as "other." Not like me. Dangerous to me, to people I love, to a country I love. But I remember that if I separate myself from anyone, I separate myself from God. How can I open my heart and feel compassion for this person?

I remember that everything we do or think or say is either an expression of love or a call for love. I drop the label.

Nothing in this section is intended as a political statement or as anything disrespectful to our brave men and women in uniform. I seek only to share some of my own struggle to see everyone as a child of God.

People with clenched fists cannot shake hands.
—INDIRA GANDHI

There Is No "Them"

Hatred never ceases by hatred, but by love alone is healed.
–Buddha

After I quoted the entire Serenity Prayer on my blog, a commenter observed that the overtly Christian language in the latter part of the prayer would be off-putting to "nonbelievers." I felt sad when I read this because the sentiment behind the prayer is lovely, at least to me, and has value beyond the limiting vocabulary of a particular faith.

In 2011, a minister in Florida burned a Koran as a statement of judgment against Islam. That, in turn, sparked retaliatory protests and killings in Afghanistan. All because we separate ourselves with different labels, different names for what we hold sacred. I don't think the universal essence, for obvious lack of better words, is so easily described, explained, or contained.

I read in Wayne Dyer's book *Inspiration* about an ancient Hindu saying that "the name of God is truth." Truth is beyond labels. The *Tao Te Ching* says, "The way that can be told is not the eternal Way. The name that can be named is not the eternal name. The nameless is the beginning of heaven and earth. The named is the mother of ten thousand things." Perhaps the labels are the mother of ten thousand beliefs, each of which distinguishes "us" from "them."

It's like speaking different languages. We can say the literal same words in English, Arabic, and Chinese, but in each language, the meaning might be different because of different cultures. Yet, like H_2O, which can take the form of water, vapor, or ice and yet retain its same molecular makeup, the words identify the same essential concept. As long as we need words to communicate, communication will be limited by those words. Communication with words will always be imperfect. We have the choice to see this imperfection as creating barriers, or we can see this imperfection as an invitation to look beyond the differences and transcend the barriers.

When this same Florida minister threatened to burn the Koran in 2010, my church bought one hundred Korans and worked with a local bookstore to give copies away to anyone who wanted one. We thought that reading the Koran might lead to better understanding and communication than burning it.

For myself, my spiritual life is enriched and deepened by embracing truth as I find it, wherever I find it. When asked one time to identify three people who influenced my faith, I named three people who, I believe, were true people of God. One was the minister of my church. One was a Buddhist monk I met in Thailand. The third was the Muslim guard who watched over my home in West Africa.

My faith community is Christian, and I have worshiped in Thai temples. I am an ordained Stephen Minister, and I am training as a Shambhala warrior. I follow Jesus and the Noble Eightfold Path of Buddhism. I have lit incense at a Hindu shrine, and I smiled as my young son bowed to Allah alongside the Muslim guard he loved.

I pray to God, Kuan Yin, Mary (when I need to talk mom to mom), the creek by my cabin (which sometimes talks back), and occasionally my dog Sam, who died years ago. When my mother died, I prayed Jewish prayers of mourning. I believe that my prayers all go to the same destination no matter how they are addressed.

My point is not to shock or alienate anyone, and I'm sorry if I have. My point is that I hope we don't close our minds to beauty because of a label. I hope we don't let language hold us back when we try to communicate about our deepest selves. If we speak our truth to one another with an open heart, and if we hold the words we hear with sacred respect, then we will surely meet in that place where there is no "them"; there is only us.

> *Imagine there's no countries*
> *It isn't hard to do*
> *Nothing to kill or die for*
> *And no religion too*
> *Imagine all the people*
> *Living life in peace...*
> *You may say I'm a dreamer*
> *But I'm not the only one*
> *I hope someday you'll join us*
> *And the world will be as one*
> —JOHN LENNON

The Perfection of Imperfection

We all have made mistakes that we remember with embarrassment and even shame. Rabbi Kushner, in his book *How Good Do We Have to Be?*, says that making mistakes is not remarkable. What is remarkable is how vivid our memories of these mistakes can be and how these memories can still trigger such intense emotion. He gives the example of missing a word in a spelling bee. He still remembers the word and how he misspelled it. I can relate. I misspelled *parade* in the fourth-grade spelling bee. I spelled it p-r-a-d-e. I can't remember whether I already gave the dog her medicine today, but I can remember how I misspelled a word half a century ago. And I'm still embarrassed about it.

I can look back over my parenting and quickly call to mind several incidents from years ago that to this day make me cringe. My chest feels tight, and I want to crawl in a hole. I pray that my children will not recall these things during their future therapy sessions, which I'm sure they will need as a result of my failings.

The memories of mistakes come unbidden and still have the power to hurt. I have to use my brain to rationally remind myself that I managed to spell enough words correctly to represent my class in the spelling bee. I have to remind myself that all five of my children have within recent memory spoken lovely words of appreciation to me.

A *Course in Miracles* teaches us that perception is a mirror, not a fact. What we perceive is our state of mind reflected outward. Rabbi Kushner says that when we define ourselves by our worst moments instead of our best, we see ourselves as never good enough rather than as good, capable people who make occasional mistakes like everybody else.

In her book *Taking the Leap*, Pema Chödrön encourages us to change our habits of perception. In every day there are moments that are not perfect as well as moments that please us. Instead of labeling the day as bleak, we can cherish the moments of joy. Gradually, we can appreciate our lives as they are, with all the ups and downs. And we can appreciate ourselves as we are, with all our imperfections.

Ernest Kurtz and Katherine Ketcham wrote, "Imperfection is...the crack in the armor, the wound that lets God in." Or more simply, I'm not okay, and you're not okay, but that's okay. It's better than okay. It's perfect.

I have no purpose for today except to look upon a liberated world, set free from all the judgments I have made.
–*A COURSE IN MIRACLES*

First Date

I read a book by Mark Hughes, the title of which begins *I Am Not a Prophet*. I was immediately attracted to the title, thinking, *I'm not a prophet, too!* We don't need to be anyone special to hear our inner guidance. The answer we seek can only be found within. And here's the good news: Everyone can find it.

Okay, okay, I get that. But maybe if I just read one more book, go to one more presentation, attend one more meditation workshop, listen to one more teacher...Maybe if I keep looking out there, I will find what I'm looking for in here. So I keep reading *about* meditation, *about* listening to my inner guidance, *about* forgiveness, *about* compassion, *about* being here now. If I keep reading *about*, perhaps I will *become*...

If I could just get to that darned nirvana place, my life would be so much better. I would be calm and joyful all the time. I would be wise. My life would be eternally blissful. I would never, ever be angry or judgmental or unhappy or even cranky. I would be a better person. A much better person.

Pema Chödrön says that this way of thinking is a subtle form of aggression (sometimes not so subtle, I think). We blame ourselves or others because of what we perceive as some lack in our own life. If it weren't for my boss, the government, my childhood, my neighbor, my ex, the terrorists, the weather, my life would be great. And my personal favorite from Pema Chödrön's list: "If it weren't for my mind, my meditation would be excellent."

No, we don't need to change anything about ourselves. We can still be our crazy, cranky, impatient, insecure, silly selves. We don't need to trade ourselves in for the new, shinier, upgraded model. Instead, we can make friends with ourselves. We can start where we are. Here. Right now.

We can start by suspending our judgments long enough to get to know who we are. Imagine that you are going out on a date with yourself. A first date. Feel the excitement and anticipation. Imagine that you are sitting across the table from yourself at your favorite restaurant (or your favorite place). What would you ask yourself? How would you answer? Treat yourself with the same curiosity and courtesy you would give your date. Have a great time!

If we befriend ourselves, we might do less searching outside and more finding inside. We might even ask ourselves for a second date!

To love oneself is the beginning of a life-long romance.
—OSCAR WILDE

From Victim to Victor

I once watched a young lawyer make his case in an appellate courtroom before a panel of three judges. The lawyer clearly had the superior legal position, and the judges kept interrupting him to assure him that they understood his argument. What they really meant was, *It's almost lunchtime and we're hungry. You've already won, so just stop.* But the lawyer was inexperienced and nervous and did not get the hints. So when he inadvertently made a misstep, the now grumpy judges pounced. They began to challenge him until he painted himself into a corner. Finally, one judge took pity and said, "Counselor, don't snatch defeat from the jaws of victory."

Our words are powerful and send out energy that calls matching energy back to us. Like an echo. A tragic example is the horrific deaths of Timothy Treadwell and his girlfriend, Amie Huguenard, who were killed in Alaska while studying bears. An audio recorder that was left running revealed that one morning a bear attacked and killed Timothy. Amie continued screaming even after the bear left. Soon after, the bear returned and killed her, too.

Experts speculated that Amie's high-pitched squeals were eerily like predator calls, devices used by hunters to lure predators out into the open. Predator calls mimic the sounds of an injured animal.

Of course, no one knows for sure whether she actually "called" the bear back to her, but we do know that our voice is an awesome gift, to be used for good or ill. We are all familiar with the concept of a self-fulfilling prophecy. While we might not be calling man-eating predators out of the shadows, we sometimes use our words, intentionally or carelessly, to send out harmful energy, which will then be reflected back to us.

We might immediately think about manipulative lies or malicious gossip or angry attacks. But what about veiled criticism and insensitive remarks? We don't always hear ourselves or realize how our words sound to others. Sometimes my daughter will blurt out whatever pops into her head, including things that hurt. When I react, she defends herself with, "But that's not what I meant," or, "I wasn't thinking." Too late.

We are even less likely to recognize the harm in voicing negative thoughts about ourselves, especially if we see the comments as funny or self-deprecating. There was a thankfully short-lived teen response to making a mistake: "Oh, I'm stupid." When any of my kids would flippantly say this, I would cringe.

We often think of words like that as harmless, even desirable. At a women's retreat I led, I was struck by how difficult it was for some women to use positive words to describe themselves. When asked to describe themselves the way they would be described by the person who loved them more than anything in the universe (this could be a parent, dearest friend, God, their dog, anyone), there was a palpable discomfort in the room. Describing themselves in glowing terms seemed not only unfamiliar but even wrong, smacking of pride and arrogance. Much better, they thought, to minimize their gifts, to deny their talents, to put themselves down.

But false modesty is just that: false. *A Course in Miracles* teaches, "Humility will never ask that you remain content with littleness. But it does not require that you be not content with less than greatness that comes not of you." Legendary martial artist Bruce Lee was once asked if he was really "that good." He replied, "If I say yes, you will think I am arrogant. But if I say no, you will know I'm lying."

The Bible says we are fearfully and wonderfully made. Far from feeling arrogant or prideful, I am brought to my knees in humility and gratitude when contemplating this precious gift of human life, a gift that is not mine alone, but is generously bestowed on each of us, binding us together in our shared magnificence. I want my thoughts and words to reflect that light of glory. The energy that we send out with shining words is indeed powerful beyond measure.

Okay, but what about the times when we really do feel stupid, incompetent, ineffective, unattractive, unsuccessful, unlovable, or unloving? We all have thoughts like that sometimes. But we don't have to give those thoughts power by voicing them. On the contrary, we can voice the opposite. We can speak the thoughts that will express and therefore attract what we want for ourselves.

As they say in Alcoholics Anonymous, "Fake it till you make it." When I suggested this in a workshop, someone objected to the concept, saying that it wasn't authentic or honest. Buddhist teacher Pema Chödrön says that's true only if we are deceiving ourselves. Rather, even "though we know exactly what we feel, we make the aspirations in order to move beyond what now seems possible."

We can choose with our words to be a victim or a victor. We can speak our greatest destiny. We can shine like stars.

Your playing small does not serve the world. There's nothing enlightened about shrinking so that other people won't feel insecure around you. We are all meant to shine, as children do....And as we let our own light shine, we unconsciously give other people permission to do the same. As we're liberated from our own fear, our presence automatically liberates others.

–MARIANNE WILLIAMSON

Step 7
Practice Compassion

If you want to make others happy, practice compassion.
If you want to make yourself happy, practice compassion.
—THE DALAI LAMA

If judgment closes our hearts, then compassion opens them. Our focus in this step is to find ways to awaken compassion, for ourselves and for others, even for the whole world. Compassion is something we can practice, and if we practice, it becomes habit.

So Generous

This link between happiness and compassion may not be immediately apparent. One dictionary definition of *compassion* is "a feeling of deep sympathy and sorrow for another who is stricken by misfortune, accompanied by a strong desire to alleviate the suffering." Frankly, this doesn't sound very happy to me.

And yet, compassion opens our hearts and connects us to others. It lifts us out of ourselves, out of our isolation and separateness, to touch with tenderness the heart of another. And there is joy in that touch.

If I were a writer of dictionary definitions, I might expand the definition of *compassion* to recognize that blurred line we sometimes experience between joy and sorrow. Tears flow as readily for one as for the other.

I heard something once that, to me, describes the raw heart of compassion. The speaker was describing the bounteous generosity of nature. The sun shines down on all without discriminating between the thief and the saint. So generous. The rain nourishes weeds as well as trees. So generous. The flowers display their beauty without regard for who is passing by. So generous.

The speaker was infinitely more eloquent than my memory allows, but the concept was much on my mind when I was at my cabin this last weekend. As I sat by the creek, I watched small insects flit above the water, visible in the sunlight, disappearing in the shadows.

The breeze sang in the trees whether I was there to hear or not. A mother duck guided her ducklings expertly through the rushing waters around rocks and under branches. It was all so exquisite. So generous.

I know, that doesn't sound anything like the definition of compassion I quoted above, but somehow it captures my experience of compassion, as both the giver and the receiver. It is the experience of a heart broken open, vulnerable, touching and touchable. Perhaps that is the essence of compassion: touch.

> *For he makes his sun rise on the evil and on the good,*
> *and sends rain on the just and on the unjust.*
> –MATTHEW 5:45

Who Are Your People?

In the South, this question is sometimes asked as a way of getting to know someone. "Who are your people?" means "Who is your family? Where are your roots? How are you connected to me, in that six-degrees-of-separation kind of way?"

I was raised in Memphis, Tennessee, but I have not lived in the South for most of my adult life. I have lived on four continents and traveled all over the world. I have now lived in the Pacific Northwest for over twenty years and call it home. But my people come from the Ozarks of Missouri. They are salt-of-the-earth people: farmers, mechanics, traders, cowboys, guitar pickers, great cooks, and a few moonshiners. And according to stories, one train robber.

When my daughter was five, I took her to a reunion in the little Ozark town where our family comes from. I have more cousins there than I can count. We checked into a tiny motel, the only one in town. We walked into our room, which was hot as Hades and had a faint odor of mildew rising from the stained shag carpet. I was trying to figure out how to crank up the window-unit air conditioner when Mia asked, "Mommy, what is this?"

I turned and saw what she was holding. "Sugar, that's how you know you are in a first-class deluxe establishment. That is a fly swatter."

While we waited for other kinfolk to show up, we moseyed across the road to the Walmart. As soon as we walked into the store, I saw my cousin Jayma Sue. And there was Monty Max and Bonnie Jo and Wanda Fern. And more. Soon we were having an impromptu family reunion in the aisles. My heart was filled with the warm embrace of my heritage, and I thought with grateful affection, *These are my people.*

I saw a bumper sticker the other day that said, *All people are my people.* I was reminded of my Southern roots and the importance of knowing who your people are. Can I look at all people with that same depth of recognition and affection? After all, at some level, we all share common ancestry, don't we? All people are indeed our people.

> *Our usual concept of "us" and "them" is outdated. In its place, we need an attitude that sees all human beings as our brothers and sisters, that considers others to be part of "us."*
>
> —THE DALAI LAMA

Mushroom Experience

We are here to awaken from our illusion of separateness.
–THICH NHAT HANH

Do you know what the largest living thing on the planet is? It's not a whale. It's not a giant redwood tree. It's a mushroom!

I know, I was surprised, too. No, more than surprised. Amazed! And I was even more than amazed to find out that this humongous mushroom grows in the United States, in Oregon, the state I call home.

When I heard this incredible information, I started scanning the horizon, wondering if I could see in the distance something like a nuclear mushroom cloud that was in fact a mushroom, the mushroom that ate Oregon. But no, you can't see it. The mushroom fungus grows underground, spreading out along a network of filaments. What we enjoy in our omelets and spaghetti sauce, what we think of as separate, distinct mushrooms, is actually the fruit of one fungus.

This particular gargantuan fungus covers over 2,200 acres (about nine square kilometers) in eastern Oregon. I could pick a tiny mushroom, and someone else could pick another tiny mushroom 3.5 miles away, and both could be part of the same organism.

The more I've learned about this mushroom fungus, the more I've thought about people. Perhaps we are like that fungus, appearing to be separate, but all connected below our visual or perceptual range. We talk about oneness at a deep spiritual level. Perhaps we are a single spiritual organism, nestled safely in the dark, fertile soil of the divine, popping up here and there as individual fruits.

Perhaps when Jesus said that our actions to the "least of these" were actions "to him," he meant exactly what he said. He didn't say it was "like" or "as if" we were doing things to him. He said that what we do to others we do *to him*. Perhaps what we do to another we do to all, including ourselves, because we are all one.

You might have heard the expression that we are spiritual beings having a human experience. Perhaps we are a fungus having a mushroom experience.

> *We might refine the Golden Rule as follows:*
> *"Do good unto others because they are you."*
> –LARRY DOSSEY

Calling for Love

If we truly wish to learn, we should consider enemies
to be our best teacher!
—THE DALAI LAMA

Many studies show that our happiness is directly related to the connection we have with others. And we are only connected to others when our hearts are open. Great concept, but hard to put into practice. How many times a day do I separate myself from someone by closing my heart with anger, judgment, criticism, fear, resentment, seeing someone else as "other"? Let's face it, there are plenty of folks out there I really don't want to be connected to. So if maintaining a connection to other people is the price of admission to my happy place, I sometimes need, as Patti LaBelle sings, a new attitude.

A Course in Miracles teaches that love has no opposite. Love is all there is. (Wasn't that a line from a Beatles song? No, that was "Love is all you need." Also true.) When something happens that blocks our awareness of love's presence, we experience that separation as fear. When we feel afraid, we reflect our separation from others through negative thoughts, words, and behaviors. In reality, all we are doing is seeking reconnection. We are calling for love. Everything we do or say or think is either an expression of love, when we are connected, or a call for love, when we are separated. Everything is one or the other. Everything. It's that simple.

When I remember this, I find that it is much easier to keep my heart open. For example, if someone is unkind to me, instead of reacting defensively, I can take a deep breath and think, *Man, you are seriously calling for love.* Someone cuts me off in traffic? *Hey, I see you are needing some love over there.* Big hurts, little affronts, it's all the same. If it isn't an expression of love, it's a call for love.

This reframing shifts my attention from my own hurt feelings or irritation. My ego is not engaged. I can stay connected at that sacred level and respond with an expression of love. This doesn't necessarily mean that I voice affection. I might smile, or simply send a silent blessing.

If I am unable to make this shift, if I react with separating thoughts or words or deeds of my own in retaliation, then later I can see that I was calling for love myself. And yes, sometimes I am the perpetrator who initiates the call for love by being unkind or insensitive to someone else. When I see my own behavior in this light, it is easier for me to accept responsibility and apologize.

Characterizing negative thoughts, words, or behavior as a call for love helps me avoid judging and reacting. If I can reinterpret a perceived attack, from myself or someone else, as a call for love, then my heart stays soft and open. Compassion flows naturally from an open heart. We stay connected and happier, and our lives become expressions of love.

> *The opposite of love is fear, but what is all-encompassing can have no opposite.*
> –A COURSE IN MIRACLES

Practicing Compassion

Go out into the world today and love the people you meet.
–MOTHER TERESA

I read a blog post recently that has been churning in my mind and spirit ever since. The title of the post was "Is My Dad in Heaven or Hell?" The writer's father had died years before in a car accident. She had since found Jesus and became very concerned about where her dad was spending eternity. She went to her minister seeking comfort. What do you think that minister said?

"Yes, your dad is in hell."

Wow.

I'm not going to get into a theological discussion, much as I'm tempted to. I'm not here to debate whether there is a heaven or a hell, or who gets to go where, or if there is any person on this earth who knows for a fact the answer to any of these questions. I'm not even here to discuss a minister's counseling skills.

What I am here to do is to confess that I am having a hard time feeling compassion for this minister. In fact, I have been full of judgment and outrage and despair over what, to me, is a perversion on so many levels of a faith that I love.

If I believe that judgment and anger separate us from others and that any separation from others is a separation from God, and I do, then I want to find a way to mend that broken connection. As I was pondering this, I noticed, really noticed, perhaps for the first time, the first word. *Practice.* Okay, so perhaps compassion is a skill I can actually practice. And perhaps I can get better at it.

Of course, I would like to get better at it *fast.* It's easy to feel compassion for the bereaved daughter. I don't need to practice feeling compassion for people who are vulnerable and hurt, for hungry children, for animals in distress. Compassion springs forth naturally when a story touches our hearts and breaks them open. The real practice occurs when compassion does not spontaneously arise, when aversion or anger or fear has closed our hearts and separated us from someone we have labeled as "other."

If I believe that all people are beloved children of God, and I do, then how do I claim my kinship with the minister who withholds comfort from an aggrieved daughter, who presumes to stand in judgment over a beloved father?

If I believe that everything we do or think or say is either an expression of love or a call for love, and I do, then this minister's words, surely not an expression of love, are necessarily and just as surely a call for love. Perhaps not a conscious call, or even an unconscious one. Rather, a spirit's call to be reconnected to all that is good and light and loving. When I characterize his words in this way, I feel my perspective shift, my tension ease, my heart soften. And in this moment, my spirit responds and sends a blessing his way.

> *My brother, peace and joy I offer you that I may have*
> *God's peace and joy as mine.*
> —A Course in Miracles

It's Oneness, Beloved

If, as Stephen Covey says, "The main thing is to keep the main thing the main thing," then I want to know what my main thing is.

I can identify guiding principles in my life, such as the practices listed in the 10 Steps, but what is the main thing that ties them all together? Like Frodo's ring in *The Lord of the Rings*. To paraphrase: One main thing to rule them all, one to find them, one to bring them all, and in the light bind them.

When asked to describe his religion, the Dalai Lama replied, "My religion is kindness." That's his main thing.

When I contemplated the theme of my guiding principles, what finally emerged was the concept of oneness. The concept that we are at our core one, one with each other, one with all life, one with God.

A Course in Miracles teaches that all suffering comes from our mistaken perception of separation. When we separate ourselves from each other, we separate ourselves from God. Jesus said that when we serve others, we serve him. We are to love our neighbors as ourselves. The Bodhisattva vow is to remain incarnated until all sentient beings are enlightened. The Marines leave no man behind.

Someone once asked, "Do we breathe, or are we being breathed?" Perhaps there is a divine Oneness breathing life into all living things. We are all joined by this single breath.

Bill Clinton became president by keeping the main thing the main thing. On the wall of his campaign headquarters was a big sign that shouted, "It's the economy, stupid!"

I think my sign whispers, *It's oneness, beloved.*

Perhaps this is why I love the greeting *namaste*, which can be translated as:

> The divine in me salutes the divine in you.
> I honor the place in you where the entire universe resides.
> I honor the place in you of Love, of Light, of Truth, of Peace.
> I honor the place in you where if you are in that place in you and I am in that place in me, there is only one of us.

Kuan Yin Calling

One Sunday morning years ago, I was driving through a business district in Portland. Everything was closed, the street deserted. I drove past a store window full of Asian ceramics and furniture. I don't like to shop. I never browse. And if I'm going somewhere, I rarely get sidetracked. But as I drove past the store, I felt a sudden urge to go in. I dismissed it and continued on, mentally noting the location for future reference. But the urge grew more insistent, almost like a scene in a Western where the cowboy lassoes the girl or bandit and reels them in. I shook it off, reminding myself that the store was no doubt closed and I had other things to do. I told myself I would come back another time.

Not good enough. The farther I drove from the store, the more compelling the urge became until finally, feeling like a crazy person, I circled back and pulled up in front. Although there were no cars in sight, there were two people standing by the door. I rolled down the window and asked if the store was open. They said they had no idea; they were just passing by.

Feeling more foolish by the second, I parked and went to the door, which, amazingly, was unlocked. I walked in and, seeing no one, called hello. A petite, elegant Chinese woman came out from the back and assured me that the store was open. She added that there were also things upstairs and downstairs. She invited me to look around and went back to whatever she had been doing.

I have always been attracted to Asian art and decor, even before I lived in Bangkok. If you came to my home, you would see rugs from China and Nepal, tapestries from Burma, furniture from Thailand, and art from all over Asia. But I had no room for more. Several closets were already full of paintings I had no wall space for in my small house. I wandered aimlessly about the store, going upstairs to see the furniture displays and then downstairs where things were seemingly haphazardly stored.

I started back upstairs to the ground level to leave, still puzzled about what drew me there in the first place. Then I saw her, a statue of Kuan Yin, covered with dust, in the midst of piled-up chairs and pillows, smiling serenely, unperturbed by her jumbled surroundings.

Her name is spelled many ways and there are many explanations of who she is but, most simply, she is identified as the goddess of mercy and compassion. Her name is sometimes translated as "the one who hears the cries of the world." She is often depicted holding a vase containing the nectar of compassion, which she pours over the world to ease suffering.

Kuan Yin and I go way back. My history with her is too long to tell right now, but I think of her as my guardian angel. So there I was, in the basement of this store, facing this exquisitely beautiful but huge bronze statue of Kuan Yin. Reminding myself of all my things I already didn't have room for, I took one last look and turned to walk away...

She now sits on a sturdy wooden table in the corner of my living room. She is the first thing anyone sees when entering the front door. I like to think she is blessing all who come, bringing peace to our troubled hearts, pouring her nectar of compassion over our spirits to ease our suffering.

So generous.

Compassion is revolution.

—BUMPER STICKER

Mary Was a Real Mother

I know a woman whose son died in a carelessly started cabin fire when he was twelve. That was twenty years ago. She told me her story after I commented on her brilliantly colored tattoo featuring her son's name and turquoise rays of light emanating from an eagle, his favorite bird. One ray embraced a heart with a piece missing.

As I listened to her story, I was struck by two things. First, you can talk to someone for a long time, years in this case, without having any idea about that person's deep story. The story that matters. Second, tragedy is both personal and universal. I have grieved and still grieve over my son's autism. Chronic grief. It is not the same as her grief, which was heart-exploding catastrophic. I can't imagine hers. She perhaps can't imagine mine. But we share a mother's broken heart.

I have often felt guided and protected by Kuan Yin, the Chinese goddess of mercy and compassion. But Kuan Yin is always serene, never born as a human being, never suffering as a mother. So when my heart has been torn apart with pain that seems unbearable, I turn to Mary, mother of Jesus. As a therapist once said to me, "She was a *real* mother." Mary is often portrayed with a radiant, sublimely loving face, a Kuan Yin face. But I don't think that is what her face really looked like much of the time.

What did her face look like when her wayward preteen disappeared, only to be found days later teaching in the temple, shrugging his shoulders at his parents' worried consternation? Or when he refused to acknowledge her in front of the crowd, instead claiming the people around him as his family? (I remember telling my mom once that I wished the nextdoor neighbor was my mom. She promptly told me to go see if Mrs. Beasley wanted any more children and locked me out of the house.)

What did Mary's face look like when her son was being ridiculed and hated? Not a mother's proudest moment. What did she answer when all the moms got together to brag about their kids and asked her, "And what does your son do?"

I'm sure none of that compared to what her face looked like as her son was arrested, tortured, and killed right in front of her. I don't care how strong your faith is. That is not something any mother should have to endure. And yet so many have. Before yielding to God's will, Jesus asked for the cup to pass from him. How many times did Mary pray this prayer? How many times have I?

I don't pretend to understand the meaning of such suffering. Or of any suffering, for that matter. But I know that some of my most fervent prayers have been to Mary. The mom prayers. The prayers a mother would understand.

I asked Mary to watch over my two too-young daughters when they were expecting babies of their own. I asked Mary to strengthen them with courage, to soften them with kindness, to inspire them with wisdom, to delight them with joy, to calm them with patience, to awaken them with compassion, to sustain them with faith. I ask the same for me.

No, I'm not Catholic, but I think that's okay with her. After all, Mary was a real mother.

> *When I find myself in times of trouble,*
> *Mother Mary comes to me, Speaking words of wisdom,*
> *Let it be.*
> —JOHN LENNON, PAUL MCCARTNEY

Finding Love

If you're feeling helpless, help someone.
–Aung San Suu Kyi

Okay, we're all suckers for sweet animal stories with cute pictures. I was browsing in the bookstore and saw this book about unusual animal friends. Animals that were natural enemies had somehow bypassed the normal circuits and were best friends: A lion and a goat. A gorilla and a kitten. A pig and a tiger.

A while back, I discovered the website for Wild Rose Rescue Ranch, a haven for injured or lost wild animals. One of their residents is a one-legged pigeon named Noah with a heart the size of the ocean. Some of his neighbors at the ranch, abandoned newborn rabbits, were dying one by one. Then one day, the human caretakers couldn't find the bunnies; there weren't even bodies. Where were they? They were nestled snugly, alive, under Noah's wings. All of those bunnies survived into adulthood.

Browsing elsewhere on the website I found this wisdom: "Love is found where love is given." I think the people who run this ranch must find love every day. Certainly Noah the pigeon does!

He will cover you with his feathers and under his wings
you will find refuge.
–Psalm 91:4

How We See Ourselves

My favorite bagger at the grocery store is David. David is a man with some sort of developmental disability, although he functions with a high degree of independence. He is unfailingly friendly, and we always chat while he is bagging the groceries. We often talk football, and he especially enjoys teasing me about my team, which is currently, well, underperforming, while his, of course, is not.

My two adult sons, James and Dan, have autism. They are not able to live independently. They are both verbal but have limited communication skills and pretty much no social sensitivity. Neither of them would be able to hold David's job. While we were together at the checkout stand recently, Dan sensed something different about David. In his usual direct way, Dan asked him, "Are you disability?"

I suppressed a gasp and glanced at Tina, the cashier. David, looking like a deer in the headlights, stammered, "What?"

Dan, bless his heart, didn't miss a beat and asked him again.

David, embarrassed, stammered yes. Tina and I quickly changed the subject, and we moved through the awkward moment with a shrug and a laugh. When I was back in the car with Dan and James, I explained to Dan that it was not polite to ask someone if they are disabled.

Dan said, as he usually does when corrected, "Oh, I'm sorry." Of course, he had no idea what I really said and will do the same thing at the next opportunity.

Then, out of curiosity and in clear violation of what I had just said, I asked Dan if he was disabled.

Without hesitation, he answered confidently, "No!"

Well, there you go, I thought. *Aren't we all like that?* I chuckled and patted Dan on the knee, and home we went.

True wisdom comes to each of us when we realize how little we understand about life, ourselves, and the world around us.

—Socrates

The Best We Can

We cannot despair of humanity, since we ourselves are human beings.
—Albert Einstein

At the beginning of each academic year, the head of my department conducted a training session for our teaching assistants, upper-level students who would be working with new students. He told them that they were likely to review some assignments that were below acceptable standards. He cautioned them that although it might look like a student had not made much of an effort, they should assume instead that all students were doing the very best they could.

At a family dinner for his brother's birthday, my son James was being deliberately, I believed, rude, choosing to disrupt the celebration at least partly because it wasn't his own birthday. I was frustrated by his unwillingness to accept my efforts to redirect his energy. I was angry. My feelings were hurt. And I was disappointed. I wanted the dinner to be a happy family time, and I wanted Dan to feel special on his special day.

Yes, I know that an inability to consider other people's feelings is a classic characteristic of James's autism. Yes, I know that he loves his birthday and has a hard time celebrating someone else's birthday. Yes, I know he likes to make animal sounds and be loud. I still thought he was knowingly and purposefully being mean.

A few days later, I visited with a friend who was, like me, struggling to understand the behavior of a family member. We talked about how hard it is not to judge. Then she sighed and said about her own family member, "Maybe she's doing the best she can." I paused and admitted, "And maybe James is doing the best he can."

Pema Chödrön wrote, "No one knows what it takes for another person to open the door." The Native Americans understood about walking a mile in someone else's moccasins. If I look at James's behavior and consider the possibility that he is doing the best he can at any given moment, then perhaps I can loosen my grip on my judgment and resentment. Perhaps I can sense a glimmer of compassion.

Perhaps I could even do that with myself. I usually take James in stride, but sometimes I am not patient or wise or understanding. Sometimes the way I wish things were runs right into the wall of the way things are. I crash and burn. Then I feel guilty and inept. But maybe, just maybe, I am doing the best I can.

Not everything we find is what we want. But if we befriend what is within us and are willing to learn from it, serenity will ultimately reign at the center of our being.

—JOYCE RUPP

Guided Tour

Recently, a childhood friend who had lived across the street from me in Memphis visited me. We had not seen each other since our early teens and had not been in touch until last year, when our paths crossed in cyberspace.

He now lives in New Orleans and, until this visit, had never been in the Northwest, which is about as far away from New Orleans in every sense as one can get in the continental United States. So for three days, I gave him his first impression of the place I have called home for twenty years. I wanted him to see the beautiful scenery, of course, but I also wanted him to understand something of the culture here, the inner workings of this city and this region.

Although I never take my life here for granted, being a tour guide for a newcomer gave me the opportunity to look at my home with fresh eyes, to voice what I appreciate about living here, to share my enthusiasm about my life here. As the days went by, I found myself more consciously aware of what was best about the place. Oh, there are faults, to be sure, and I didn't deny them, but I wanted to put my city's best foot forward, so to speak. As I did so, I was filled with tenderness and love and gratitude for this community that welcomed me with open arms all those years ago.

It occurred to me that we might awaken this same tenderness and compassion for ourselves by a similar process. Many guidebooks include sections on history, culture, places to see, and things to do. A guide book for our lives could include these same sections. My hope is that a fresh look at our lives in this way will awaken compassion for ourselves. There is a saying that charity begins at home. Compassion does, too. Experiencing compassion and appreciation for ourselves will spill over to others as well.

> *You yourself, as much as anybody,*
> *deserve your love and affection.*
> –THE DALAI LAMA

In the Softness

Underneath the hardness there is fear
Underneath the fear there is sadness
In the sadness there is softness
In the softness is the vast blue sky
—Unknown

Lately, that poem's last line has been floating in my spirit like a fluffy cloud on a balmy day. I have written about feeling regret over how I handled my early parenting years. Even bigger than the regret is the sadness, the deep spirit sadness of ungrieved grief.

When my son James was a baby, he was so beautiful. Everything seemed possible. Over time, it was clear to everyone but me that something was different about him, something to be concerned about. But I saw only magical uniqueness. Even when he was diagnosed with autism, I failed to acknowledge or to accept the loss of my dreams. I failed to see him for, yes, the truly magically unique child he was. I denied the impact on my heart and on my life, and set out to force a brittle façade of happy normalcy on us all. The alternative was simply more than I could bear.

With the arrival of my grandson Jaden, whose looks remind me so much of James when he was a baby, memories have resurfaced. And with those memories, some of the feelings have resurfaced, too. This time, however, I am not afraid. Feelings that I rejected before are now welcomed. Sadness is tenderly cradled.

In that sadness there is softness. A sweet softness. My daughter, Jaden, James, and I went out to dinner last night. I looked from Jaden's laughing baby face to James's laughing grown-up face and thought of all the years, all the years of loving James so much, of hurting so much, of wanting so much. All the years of being so afraid.

I marveled at the cosmic wisdom of timing. What seemed so terrifying all those years ago seems strangely comfortable now. What I tried to hide is now precious. And what I felt so angry about I am now profoundly grateful for. Of all my children, James broke my crusty heart open. And we all know what brilliant rainbow beauty sparkles inside the dull geode shell.

There will always be a raw tenderness in my heart for James, a place sensitive to touch. A place of quiet grieving. And that's okay. The grief I denied all those years ago is now free. I breathe into the softness of it, trusting in the basic goodness of the universe, the perfection of it all, the sunny brightness of the vast blue sky.

So now faith, hope, and love abide, these three;
but the greatest of these is love.
—1 CORINTHIANS 13:13

Step 8

Forgive Everyone

To forgive is to set a prisoner free and discover
that the prisoner was you.
—Lewis B. Smedes

Forgiveness is a challenging practice, the hardest of the 10 Steps for many of us. It is related to Step 3, because forgiveness requires us to let go of what we are trying to control. We have to let go of how we wanted things to be in the past, or how we want things to be in the present. When we look deeper, we'll see that the main obstacle to forgiving others is forgiving ourselves.

The F Word

No, not that F word. The other F word. *Forgiveness.* Forgiveness is a central idea in the Bible. And in *A Course in Miracles.* In psychology. In twelve-step programs. It is central to Amish culture. Although I'm no expert, I'm guessing it is central in other faith traditions and self-development programs as well. People read thousands of books about it, spend years in therapy to be able to give it or receive it. People beg for it, offer it, pray for it, resist it, marvel at it, long for it, fear it.

Most everyone agrees that forgiveness is a good thing. Some people think there are those who should not be forgiven. They would withhold forgiveness from someone who expresses no remorse, who is a repeat offender, or who does something so horrible that forgiveness seems out of the question.

I believe they likely confuse forgiveness with reconciliation, self-protection, or trivialization—all focused on the wrongdoer. But forgiveness isn't about the forgiven; it's about the forgiver. Withholding forgiveness separates us from others, which inevitably results in fear, which in turn is often masked as judgment. It is, as the saying goes, like drinking rat poison and hoping the rat will die.

Well, goshdarnit, if withholding forgiveness is so toxic, and forgiving is so beneficial, why is it so hard to do? And do we really have to forgive *everyone*? Yes, even ourselves.

Let's pay attention to what happens in our bodies when we think about forgiving someone. Perhaps our heart is beating a little faster, or our head is starting to hurt, or our throat is closing up, or our brain is spinning. That's okay. We can take a few belly breaths and let it go for now. Just be aware.

> *Who could be set free while he imprisons anyone? A jailer is*
> *not free, for he is bound together with his prisoner.*
> —A COURSE IN MIRACLES

A Child Will Lead Them

Father, forgive them, for they know not what they do.
—LUKE 23:34

Sometimes we come face-to-face with forgiveness in all its raw demand, and powerful promise. In 1960, federal marshals escorted Ruby Bridges to her first-grade class. She was the only black student sent to integrate an all-white school in New Orleans. Onlookers could see her mouth moving, saying something as she walked, so tiny inside the circle of towering marshals, through the raging crowd screaming every vile thing you can imagine and some you likely can't. Later, when asked what she was saying, she said that she was praying, praying that she would be strong and not afraid, and praying for God to forgive the people in the crowd because they didn't know what they were doing. Ruby was six years old.

Have you ever apologized to a child? "Sorry, honey, I forgot," or, "I should not have said that," or, "I'll make it up to you." How quickly did the child respond with forgiveness? The younger the child, the more quickly he forgives, it seems. The wrong that I would have nursed a grudge over for months is almost immediately shrugged off.

What do children know about forgiveness that we've forgotten? How many petty affronts, real or imagined, have you held on to long past the expiration date? Perhaps holding an image of the little Ruby in your mind will help you let go. Instead of forgiving those who have wronged you, ask forgiveness for holding on to your righteous arrogance.

Please, God, forgive me, because I don't know what I'm doing.

The wolf will live with the lamb, the leopard will lie down with the goat, the calf and the lion and the yearling all together, and a little child will lead them.

–ISAIAH 11:6

From the Ashes

*Forgiveness is the fragrance that the violet sheds
on the heel that has crushed it.*
–MARK TWAIN

On October 2, 2006, Charles Carl Roberts IV held ten Amish girls hostage in their one-room schoolhouse in Nickel Mines, Pennsylvania. He tied them up and lined them up against the wall. There was evidence that he planned to sexually assault them, but upon the quick arrival of state troopers, he decided to just start killing. The oldest girl, only thirteen, asked to be shot first, hoping that some extra time might save her friends. He shot her first. Then he shot them all, killing five, and finally shot himself.

Imagine being one of those girls. Imagine being one of their parents. I can't. But if the crime itself was unfathomable, then even more so was the response of the Amish community. Within hours of the shooting, a grandfather of one of the slain girls was heard admonishing others not to hate the shooter or to think evil of him. They quickly reached out to his family and offered forgiveness and condolences. They attended his funeral and invited his widow to attend the funeral of one of the girls. They invited her and her children, the children of the man who murdered their own children, to become members of their community.

The accounts of forgiveness flashed around the world. I read everything I could read about it and found websites in many countries marveling at a faith that most of us would believe beyond human capacity. Certainly beyond my own. I knew I was witnessing a gift. Even a miracle. The response of a small group of previously unknown people to an unimaginable tragedy inspired millions to examine their own hearts, to consider, if only for a moment, the possibility of transcendence.

The following year I read a book titled *Amish Grace*, in which the authors put the community's response in the context of their faith culture, in which forgiveness is a central concept. It permeates the way they interact with each other, raise their children, and live their lives. The author made it clear that the Amish do not equate forgiveness with lack of consequences. Had the shooter lived, they would have supported whatever justice the legal system imposed...and then visited him in prison.

Many of these particular Amish people, when questioned about their practice of forgiveness, replied with puzzlement, "Amish forgiveness is just Christian forgiveness." One person, after hesitating a moment, wondered, "Is it different from Christian forgiveness?" Is it? Is it different from the concept of forgiveness in any other faith? It appears to be so universally fundamental. And yet we struggle so to live it.

What would our lives look like if we could forgive like that? What would our communities look like? Our world? Can we consider the possibilities for just a moment? Imagine.

Forgiveness is not an occasional act; it is a permanent attitude.
—MARTIN LUTHER KING JR.

Righteous Unforgiveness

Everyone says forgiveness is a lovely idea,
until they have something to forgive.
–C. S. Lewis

Have you ever noticed how some of the greatest advocates for forgiveness are among those who have the greatest reasons to remain bitter?

The Amish community forgave the man who came into one of their schoolhouses and shot ten little girls, killing five of them.

Nelson Mandela forgave his jailers and healed his country through truth and reconciliation.

Ruby Bridges prayed for God to forgive the screaming throngs hurling racist threats at her as she walked into her newly integrated school.

There are many stories of Holocaust survivors who refused to hate, of POWs from Vietnam who went back and met with their captors, of victims of horrific crimes who forgave the perpetrators.

And then there's me. When I was a girl, I was playing ball one day with the neighbor's children in their front yard. I saw one of the kids cheating, and I called him on it. His siblings came to his defense and the shouting quickly escalated. I was relieved when my mom came outside to see what the fuss was about, certain she would take my side. Instead, she suggested that I apologize and that we go on with our game. When I refused, she issued an ultimatum: Either I would apologize, or I could never play with these kids again. Without a moment's hesitation, I stood my self-righteous ground (after all, he *was* cheating), and I never played with, or even spoke to, any of those kids again.

I shake my head when I think about it after all these years. I mean, really. And yet, if I think a little more, I bet I can come up with some folks I am holding a grudge against right now.

There is sometimes a perverse pleasure in holding a grudge. Our anger can make us feel powerful, masking our feelings of grief and helplessness. Our hurt can attract the sympathy of those who validate our victim-ness, who take our side against the one who did us wrong.

My daughter sometimes will post a Facebook message about some dispute she is having with her boyfriend. Her willingness to air her private business was a mystery to me until I saw the quick flood of responses feeding the conflict by offering sympathy for her and condemnation for him. All this from people who know little about their relationship or what really happened in each particular instance. That quick validation of our anger is heady stuff but serves only to exacerbate the hostility. We believe ourselves to be right and the other deserving of punishment. We want the other person to suffer condemnation, to be tortured by remorse, to grovel in repentance. We want justice. We want not to hurt.

Holding a grudge can be secretly delicious, like poison. I've been thinking about poison lately because, with some degree of spiritual turmoil, I've been putting out ant poison for the hordes of sugar ants invading my kitchen. The poison must be irresistible because they stream to it like parched nomads finding an oasis. They crowd around the drops of death and drink until there is no more. They take the poison back to their nest and feed it to their babies. The poison then dries up their insides, and they all die.

Unforgiveness is like that, I think. It might taste good, but it dries us up inside. No matter what our justification is for holding the grudge, we are poisoning ourselves. So the other person did something that was so terrible it's unforgivable? Doesn't matter. The other person is not sorry at all and never will be? Doesn't matter. All our friends think we're right? Doesn't matter. We are drinking poison.

Our planet is in great trouble, and if we keep carrying old grudges and do not work together, we will all die.
—CHIEF SEATTLE

God Bless that Ol' @#&'!

To be wronged is nothing, unless you continue to remember it.
–Confucius

Here is the good news: We don't have to mean our forgiveness, at least not right away. All we have to do is be willing to mean it. Or even to consider the possibility that one day we might be willing to mean it.

Some years back I blamed someone for causing me so much stress and anguish that I thought I was going to die of it. I'll call this person Fred. (If your name is Fred, or if someone you love is named Fred, I apologize, and I invite you to substitute any name you prefer.) I hated Fred. I wanted bad things to happen to him. I fantasized about terrible things I'm too ashamed to describe.

Over time, life settled down and went on. But my fury still burned brightly. I thought about it and talked about it. A lot. Until finally, I was tired of it. Tired and bored. I groaned and rolled my eyes every time I heard myself telling the story again. And again. And *again*. Goodness knows how my friends stood me. I eventually couldn't stand myself.

I knew that my not forgiving was costing me my well-being—physically, emotionally, spiritually. I began to want to change. I thought I could just decide to forgive and be done with it. That didn't work. I read books on forgiveness. I did workbooks on forgiveness. But I was stuck. I obsessively and repeatedly revisited all the wrongs I thought

I had suffered at the hands of Fred, like watching news accounts of some horrible crime or natural disaster over and over. It was an addiction—a habit I couldn't stop.

My brain was in a rut. A rut worn so deep from driving over it a gazillion times that I couldn't steer out of it. I needed to start building a new path. My brain needed a new habit. So this is what I did:

Every time I thought about Fred, at the very instant I began to repeat my habitual pattern, I substituted a new thought before the emotions started churning. Before I was hooked. "God bless Fred, and please help me mean it." Let me be clear. I did not mean it. Not for a second. I did not mean the "God bless Fred" part, and sometimes I didn't even mean the "please help me mean it" part.

But the point really wasn't to mean it. At least not yet. The point was to break the habit. To get out of the rut. And perhaps to ask for help.

So I prayed this prayer over and over. At the beginning, sometimes several times an hour. Many times a day. And over weeks and months, very slowly, the blame loosened its grip. My heart began to soften. My feelings didn't boil when a thought about Fred crossed my mind. The thoughts didn't come so often. By then, the prayer had become a habit, so that when a thought of Fred popped up, the blessing was automatically triggered. Sometimes I hardly noticed it. And finally one day I said it and gasped in amazement. I really did mean it. I really, truly wished Fred well. It was a miracle.

Forgiveness is not an act of will. It is an act of willingness, a willingness that opens the crack in our hardened heart shell just enough so that we can breathe in the healing power of compassion and breathe out the toxic tar of bitterness. The moment we entertain the possibility of being willing to forgive, our course is set, and forgiveness is on the way.

The only thing harder than forgiveness is the alternative.
—PHILIP YANCEY

Dog Is God Spelled Backward

Sadie's face and paws are white with age. She has fatty lumps under her skin, and unattractive moles around her eyes. The teeth she has left are stained, and her breath is bad. She is deaf as a post, and that makes her skittish, so she barks a lot. Her voice is damaged, and her bark sounds like a soft, hoarse woof. When she gets up, her back legs are stiff, and she sometimes falls. Her digestive system is, shall we say, delicate.

I think back over fourteen years of her companionship. She has been my constant buddy, even going to work at the law school with me. She sleeps with me. She starts the night at the foot of the bed, but she ends it leaning over me like Snoopy over Charlie Brown and pokes me with her paw until I lift up the covers and she scoots under, curling up behind my knees.

I think back to her puppy days, when my children were people puppies. My daughter would dress her up and put her in the doll stroller. Sadie would look at me with mournful eyes as I laughed and took photos. James would dance with her. She was happiest when we were all at home. She always had a person to lean up against, confirming the description of her breed as Velcro dogs.

I've not always been as good to her as she has been to me. There have been days too cold or rainy for my liking, so the leash remained on top of the refrigerator. There have been times when the ball dropped by my feet repeatedly has just as repeatedly been ignored. There have been times when I impatiently hurried her along when smells too bewitching to resist beckoned from the foliage.

And yet she has never turned her back on me. She has never been cranky or irritable. She has never ignored my overtures of affection. She overlooks my shortcomings and dismisses my imperfections. She is always glad to see me and is always sad to see me go. As many times as I have failed her, she has forgiven me, without hesitation and without asking for an apology. She never brings up my past transgressions.

Her forgiveness is as pure and generous as a child's. Without judgment or complaint. She reflects back to me a vision of myself as lovable and loved.

What could I possibly have done to deserve such grace? Nothing.

Oh Lord, help me be the person my dog thinks I am.
                                                    –Unknown

Giving by Asking

Forgiveness is giving up all hope of having had a better past.
—Anne Lamott

I told the story earlier in this chapter about Fred, a person I struggled mightily and long to forgive. Even after I had come to mean the blessings I was asking God to bestow upon Fred, I realized that I had only completed half the work of forgiving. I still saw myself as the innocent party in this story. I had heaped judgment and blame on Fred. I had wished unpleasant things for him. And I had completely denied my own contribution to the escalation of the enmity between us. It was *my own reaction to what had happened* that created such a monster of bitterness and anger. It was my own feeding of that resentment that caused forgiveness to take so long and require so much effort.

I myself had committed hurtful thoughts, words, and actions, both during the time of conflict and for a long time afterward as I nursed my fury and pain. And so in my heart, I asked Fred for forgiveness. It wasn't easy. I didn't like admitting, even to myself, the things I had thought and said and done. Humbling, to be sure.

I'm wondering if I have stumbled onto a shortcut to forgiving others. Giving forgiveness is easier if you are also asking for forgiveness. It is very difficult to ask for forgiveness and judge someone at the same time. That's because asking for forgiveness is a heart-opening gesture. By shifting our attention, even momentarily, from blaming the other person to looking for our own responsibility, we soften the hardness of our hearts. We see that we are in need of forgiveness, too.

Even the honest attempt to search for our own contribution to a problem ... helps to break through the narrow patterns of thinking that lead to ... so much discontent in ourselves and in the world.

—THE DALAI LAMA

Forgiveness Sometimes Just Happens

Call it serendipity. Call it coincidence. Call it cosmic intervention. I think I'll just call it a miracle.

Eight years ago, in the spring, I had a falling out with someone I had been close friends with for two decades. There were misunderstandings, hurt feelings, anger, and perceived betrayal on both sides. After a final exchange of e-mails and phone calls, communication ceased.

I missed this friendship so much. Over the years, the sharp pain became a dull ache but never went away. Every spring I would think about what happened, and the hurt and grief would be stirred up again.

A few weeks ago, as we celebrated my son's twenty-fifth birthday, he and I were reminiscing about his childhood. He remembered some of the friends he played with and, to my surprise, he mentioned my ex-friend's daughter, although they had only seen each other a couple of times when he was very young. Then, a couple of weeks after the birthday, I received two computer-generated e-mails from my old friend's company. I had never been on its e-mail list before.

I took a chance yesterday and sent an e-mail. I said that I missed our friendship and that I was sorry for whatever mistakes I made that contributed to our estrangement. I did not ask for a response. I simply sent my best wishes.

I didn't expect a response at all and certainly not a favorable one, so I was truly surprised to get an almost immediate reply, echoing my sadness over our lost friendship and wishing to reconnect. And so, this morning, we spent an hour on the phone, catching up on family news and describing our current lives. Neither of us brought up the issue that had split us apart. It didn't seem important, and we were enjoying each other's voices and laughter too much.

I don't know what will happen. I don't know if we will stay in touch and, if so, what that will be like. I don't know if we will feel the need to go back over what happened and listen to each other's heart. But I know I'm glad I listened to that gentle inner nudge to reach out. I know that today's conversation lightened my spirit and released the regret that I have carried all these years.

Without ever speaking the words, I forgave and I felt forgiven. It just happened. So amazing. So generous.

Let me forgive and be happy.
–A COURSE IN MIRACLES

The Unkindest Cut

For Brutus, as you know, was Caesar's angel.
Judge, O you gods, how dearly Caesar lov'd him!
This was the most unkindest cut of all;
For when the noble Caesar saw him stab,
Ingratitude, more strong than traitors' arms,
Quite vanquish'd him: then burst his mighty heart.
—SHAKESPEARE

Have you ever done anything unforgivable? Has anyone done anything against you that you think is forever unforgivable?

Who are our favorite targets of eternal damnation? Perhaps an ex. Parents, of course, are often high on the list. Sometimes political or spiritual leaders who have betrayed our trust. Someone who has committed an act of violence against us or against someone we love. Someone who has hurt our children. Or any children. And, secretly perhaps, ourselves.

When we finish our list of those from whom we would withhold forgiveness, we might find that some of those at the top are people we once loved. Maybe we still do. Like Caesar, we are most vulnerable to those to whom we have exposed our tender hearts. From those, we receive the unkindest cuts of all.

Therapists' couches are populated with legions come to exorcise the demons of childhood set upon them by well-meaning or sometimes not so well-meaning parents, by bullies, by best friends gone bad. At some point, forgiveness will enter the conversation and become the key to freedom and moving on.

Not long after my mother died, I had a dream about her. In the dream, she was standing chest deep in a small pond, fully clothed. She looked confused and disoriented. She tried to move to the side of the pond to get out, but wherever she turned, she couldn't seem to reach the edge. I was standing nearby. Initially, I felt detached, like a neutral observer, but as I watched, I felt my heart slowly soften and I was filled with such deep, sad compassion. I wanted to take her in my arms and lift her up out of the water. I wanted to wrap her in warm blankets and stroke her hair and soothe her with lullabies.

When I woke up, I knew that whatever grievances I had harbored had dissolved. I saw her as she was, as we all are, perfect in her imperfection, loving in her own way, battling her own demons as best she could. A lot like me.

At some point in our lives, most of us find ourselves in our own pond of murky water, not sure how we got in there, not seeing how to get out. There are secrets lurking in the water. Draining the pond will give us a way out but will expose what we want to keep hidden. A tough choice.

A memory that still crushes my chest with shame is something that happened when my son James was two. At that time, we were living in Abidan, Ivory Coast, and we had traveled to Dakar, Senagal, where I was scheduled to participate in a panel discussion. Earlier on that day, we had taken a ferry with some friends to do some sightseeing. As we were walking along the dock to head back, I was horrified to see the ferry casting off. Somehow we had misjudged the time. Waiting till the next ferry would cause me to miss the panel.

The ferry was still close enough to the dock that other latecomers were reaching out and grabbing the rail and stepping across to board.

For me to do that, I had to hand my toddler to one of our friends already on board standing at the rail, so that my hands were free to get on board myself. I am reliving it right now, holding him out across the water while a friend reached out from the boat. I could see that she had him, but still I held on, asking her several times to assure me that she had him. She did. Letting go of him above that dark, oily water was terrifying. She clasped him in her arms while I easily took hold of the rail and jumped on board. I made it in time to the panel, but my mind was still on that dock. That moment of handing him over seared my soul like a brand.

I did much worse things than that as a mother. Things I have acknowledged and moved on from. So why is it that that scene, decades later, causes my heart to pound like the tell-tale heart of Poe? In my rational mind, I know James was not in any danger. But in my mother mind, I have a fear that in that moment I was more concerned about my being late to speak on a panel, about letting people down and the attendant embarrassment, than I was about my child.

True or not, it doesn't matter. I'll never know. But how do I forgive myself for that? The unkindest cuts of all, the ones that haunt us, are sometimes ones we inflict upon ourselves.

Love yourself—accept yourself—forgive yourself—and be good to yourself, because without you the rest of us are without a source of many wonderful things.
—LEO F. BUSCAGLIA

Radical Forgiveness

Forgiveness is the path to happiness.
—A Course in Miracles

I led a women's retreat last fall. The theme of the retreat was four radical spiritual practices that lead to radical joy. One of the practices is radical forgiveness.

What do we think of when you think of the word *radical*? Maybe the radical protesters of the sixties, radical fundamentalists, the radical left, radical change and, these days, free radicals. The word comes from the Latin word meaning "root." *Radical* can mean fundamental, or extreme, or not ordinary.

Keeping that in mind, a radical spiritual practice would be something that is not traditional. If we think about forgiveness, what does traditional forgiveness look like? We probably start by thinking that a person did something bad to us. Forgiving that person would mean releasing that person from our judgment, releasing the hold that the transgression has on our heart.

The Bible tells us we should forgive, as do many faiths and secular wisdom. But it's not easy. I can dredge up things from long ago—a best friend who hurt my feelings, a broken promise, a forgotten invitation, a betrayal of confidence—that still sting. A few years ago, someone who was upset with me about something that was happening between us right then burst forth with complaints about things I had done as a teenager. And while the accusations were valid, all I could think was, *Gosh, haven't I improved at all in the last forty years?*

What is the power these wrongs have over us? Why is it that I believe so strongly that forgiveness is a good idea and yet still nurse wounds long past? I wonder if it doesn't start with the definition of *forgive.*

The definitions I found focus on granting pardon or ceasing to blame or to resent. These definitions assume that a wrong has been committed. If it has been committed against me, then I must be a victim.

What if we question that assumption? What if no wrong has been committed? *A Course in Miracles* teaches that all perception of attack is based on a mistaken belief that we are separate from each other. Our whole view of the world is a creation of our egos, based in a past that isn't real. Forgiveness is the miracle that corrects that mistake.

Hmm, I can get my head around this sometimes, for a few moments, when I am in a very deep kumbaya place of oneness. But much of the time, I am in a world of separate people who sometimes hurt my feelings or irritate me. When I am in pain, it's hard to shift my worldview to erase perceived transgressions as though they never happened.

So, what if I could transform them? Not by traditional forgiveness, which uses a wronged-victim model, but by radical forgiveness, which is based on a victimless model that leads to gratitude. *Gratitude*: not a word we often associate with forgiveness, but let's consider it.

Here's how it might work:

1. We have to acknowledge what has happened. Tell our story and feel our feelings about it. I'll use an example from child-

hood when my best friend sided with the popular kids at a party, joining them in making fun of me and excluding me from the group. It still hurts.

2. That hurt can manifest as anger and judgment and create an obstacle to forgiveness. We can increase our suffering by trying to control what we can't control. I might want my friend to be sorry. I might want her to stand up for me and tell off all those prissy little you-know-whats. So I need to befriend my pain rather than deny it. The Buddhist monk Thich Nhat Hanh teaches us to cradle our feelings like a baby.

3. Once our pain is honored and soothed, we can begin to look below the feelings at the underlying facts. Instead of judging my friend's actions as selfish and mean, could I consider that she wanted the same things I did: to be popular, to belong, to be liked, to be accepted, to be valued? Might some of my anger toward her mask envy because she was included and I wasn't? When I start considering other interpretations, my heart softens, and I begin to feel compassion instead of condemnation.

4. Until now, we have still been using the model of the wronged victim, but here is where the radical part begins. Is it possible that what happened actually benefitted us in some way? For us to consider this, we have to loosen our grip on our victim identity. In what ways are our lives better because of what happened? What comes to mind is how that event shaped my views about inclusion. I won't claim to be always compassionate, but whenever I see anyone being left out, being teased or bullied, I don't hesitate to stand up for that person. And if I am in a group, I am more sensitive to issues of inclusion, making sure that everyone has a place at the table. As a parent, I was more attuned to these

issues in the lives of my children, helping them cope if they were the targets and imposing quick justice and education if they targeted others.

5. Thinking of that long-ago event in this light transforms my friend's actions from an attack to a gift. The pain is transformed into compassion. I am transformed from a victim to a more sensitive friend, a wiser parent, a more aware person. Forgiveness is transformed into the pearl of gratitude. And gratitude leads to joy.

It is a miracle, after all. And all miracles are radical.

You meant it for harm, but God meant it for good.
—GENESIS 50:20

For Today, Newly Bright

I have a watercolor painting in my bedroom of a tiny sparrow sitting in some tall grasses and flowers as the sun's yellow rays brighten the retreating gray of early morning. The painting is entitled "For Today, Newly Bright."

The painting reminds me every morning that today is a new day. A fresh start. A new beginning. A day of possibilities. What will I do with them?

One thing I don't want to do is haul all my old baggage into this bright, new day. Whatever is in need of forgiveness, others or me, for big mistakes or small, can weigh me down as I greet the gift of this new day.

The Dalai Lama has wise advice for starting each day. Every day, think as you wake up:

> Today I am fortunate to be alive. I have a precious human life. I am not going to waste it. I am going to use all my energies to develop myself, to expand my heart out to others, to achieve enlightenment for the benefit of all beings. I am going to have kind thoughts toward others. I am not going to get angry or think badly about others. I am going to benefit others as much as I can.

The first part focuses on gratitude. A simple thank you for our lives, an appreciation of the gift we have been given. The second part focuses on aspirations for the day. We can make whatever aspirations we want. For me, I like to release any darkness I'm hiding. I've learned that forgiveness is often not a one-time event. It is an ongoing openness, an attitude, a willingness. Sometimes I have to release resentment about the same incident over and over. It is not a linear process. It's a mindset. Or a mind reset.

Pema Chödrön describes this aspiration practice as "one at the beginning, and one at the end." In the morning, she makes an aspiration for the day. For example, "May I release everyone from blame." Then, in the evening, she reviews the day. We might not have a perfect aspiration track record for the day. Chödrön anticipates that by encouraging us to rejoice if we remember our aspiration even once during the day. And if we forgot it completely, then we can rejoice that we have the capacity to be aware of that!

I like this practice because it not only addresses lingering grudges but it also invites us to forgive ourselves for our shortcomings, real or imagined, throughout the day.

The Buddhist practice of beginning anew is a determination not to repeat the mistakes of the past, a commitment to living in mindfulness. It reminds me of the Christian concept of reconciliation and the Jewish concept of atonement. Honestly acknowledging our past frees us to begin anew. Each time we make this vow to ourselves, transformation occurs immediately. We can renew this intention as often as we feel the need to unburden our hearts and start fresh.

I like the theme of rejoicing in our effort rather than scolding ourselves for our imperfection. What a pleasant way to begin and end the day, with gratitude instead of blame. And to anticipate tomorrow. Full of promise. Newly bright.

True forgiveness is not an action after the fact, it is an attitude
with which you enter each moment.
–DAVID RIDGE

Forgiveness, the Final Frontier

Be assured that if you knew all, you would pardon all.
–Thomas à Kempis

Of all the 10 Steps, forgiveness is one of the most challenging. The foundation of so many teachings, and the subject of endless studies, it remains one of the most difficult to accomplish, and, at least for me, to write about.

"Forgive us our debts, as we forgive our debtors." Those familiar with the Christian faith recognize this as part of the Lord's Prayer. But do you know the verses immediately following the Lord's Prayer in Matthew 6:14–15? "For if you forgive others their trespasses, your heavenly Father will also forgive you, but if you do not forgive others their trespasses, neither will your Father forgive your trespasses." I guess this last part is there just in case you need it spelled out because you weren't paying attention when you were praying.

That's harsh! One person in our monthly discussion group asked in despair, "So if I can't forgive someone, then I won't be forgiven?" Yikes!

I don't think God is that stingy with forgiveness or exacts a quid pro quo. I believe that we live in a perpetual state of eternal grace. All of us, of any faith and of no faith. I don't think we can do anything to earn it or lose it. But we fallible humans become sidetracked by the merits of forgiveness. *Does this person deserve it? Do I?* We get caught up in judgment, knowing at some level we are reaping what we sow. And all the time, grace surrounds us and permeates us. It just is, like the air we breathe.

If we really understood how central forgiveness is to our well-being, to our happiness, we would practice it like our hair was on fire. My failure to forgive does not change who I am. Nor does it affect whomever it is that I am not forgiving. What it does is block my awareness of grace. I don't like my awareness of grace blocked. So I try to forgive everyone, including myself.

In *A Path with Heart,* Jack Kornfield suggests picturing every person as a Buddha, all enlightened, all here to teach us. Imagine that everything that anyone does is solely for our benefit, to help us awaken. Sometimes as I go through my day, I try this, looking at anyone I encounter, or imagining anyone I think of, as a Buddha. Inwardly, I bow in respect and say thank you.

But still, it's so hard sometimes. Even the concept is hard to grasp, like a squirming, slippery fish. Forgiveness sometimes masks judgment. As in, *I forgive you because I am a better person than you.* Or lack of compassion, as in, *I forgive you because I want you to feel guilty.* And even when we genuinely forgive someone, sometimes the forgiveness doesn't stay put. As in, *I know I forgave you for this, but I was just remembering what you did and now I'm all upset again.*

Only last night I was entertaining my daughter's boyfriend with tales of some of her youthful misdeeds, and in the telling I became agitated and angry about one particular incident, although it happened years ago and I hadn't even thought about it in ages. What started as a funny story that we were all laughing about triggered the hurt feelings like it was happening now. Wow.

So we start where we are. Sometimes that means I can enter the experience of universal grace, if only for a moment. Sometimes it means forgiving the same thing over and over. Sometimes it means that I can only express the willingness to forgive at some point in the future when I'm ready. It's all okay. Whatever tiny step we can take to soften the hard crust around our hearts, to open a crack, to momentarily shift our perception, to consider the possibility of forgiveness, is to invite grace into our awareness.

And grace, once invited, will surely come.

Let us forgive each other — only then will we live in peace.
    —LEO TOLSTOY

Step 9

Develop an Attitude
of Gratitude

*In daily life we must see that it is not happiness that makes us
grateful, but gratefulness that makes us happy.*
—David Steinal-Rast

After a challenging step about forgiveness, we can be grateful that this step is so much easier. Anne Lamott says that there are basically two prayers: "Help me, help me, help me," and "Thank you, thank you, thank you." If we pray more of the second one, we'll discover that we need less of the first one!

An Ordinary Day

"What's up?"

"Not much. What's up with you?"

"Not much."

For most of my adult life, this is not a conversation I could have had. There was always some aspect of my life in upheaval, in crisis, in dramatic transition. Much of what was hard was hard because I made hard things harder, by trying to control events and people, by trying to make things other than what they were, by never asking for or accepting help, by magical thinking and massive denial, by debilitating guilt and shame.

I used to wish for an ordinary day. A day like any other, when nothing major happened, when there was no crisis to handle. A day that was unremarkable, with no surprises, a day easy to forget.

I have days like that now. That's partly because my life has settled down a lot in recent years. And it's partly because I have learned to roll along with life a bit more smoothly than before.

When I have an ordinary day, I savor every moment. Sometimes I stop in the middle of errands or chores or just reading or watching TV, and think to myself, *I love my life so much.* I want to run up to people and shake them and say, "Are you having an ordinary day? Do you know how lucky you are?"

I try to remember to say a prayer for all the millions of people who are having a day like the ones that used to be the norm for me. And for the many more who are having a day much worse than the worst of mine. (On my worst day I had so much to be grateful for if I had only looked at things differently.)

What's up? Not much. Thank God.

Live contented.

–PAUL REVERE (INSCRIBED ON THE WEDDING RING HE GAVE HIS WIFE)

Voices in the Sea

Here are some things I've complained about recently: my clothes were not completely dry when I went to get them out of the dryer; the hummingbirds have been ignoring the alluring feeder I have hanging by the window; my computer has been acting up.

Then I read a passage in a book that stopped me in my whiny tracks. The book is *The Pursuit of Happiness* by David Myers. In one chapter, the author suggested that having a broader view puts our trivial, temporary inconveniences in perspective. He told this story from World War II:

> A British veteran reflected on his experience with things of gravest import after sailing with Russia-bound convoys through German-submarine-infested icy waters: "There are two things that I shall always remember. The first is the sound of men's voices in the sea at night, when you can't stop to pick them up... and the other is the sound of people's voices complaining in the shops at home."

When I read that, I felt so ashamed of the things I thought warranted my critical commentary. Here are some more examples. It was hot in tae kwon do class the other night. I leaned my sweaty face near a classmate's and moaned, "I'm dying in here!" Well, it *was* hot, but of course I wasn't dying. I was voluntarily engaging in an activity I truly enjoy.

The second example is a bit more complicated. The simple version is that I am struggling to get health insurance since my retirement, and I spent several conversations with friends detailing the hours I have spent in the infuriating morass of insurance runaround and outlining everything that is wrong with our health insurance system in the United States. Yes, there are problems with our system, to be sure, and there is nothing wrong with having an opinion about the pros and cons of various alternatives. But I wasn't having a reasoned discussion. I was griping, pure and simple.

The short passage from Myers's book with the stark contrast between people dying terrifying deaths and people kvetching in the store went right into my heart. Perhaps because I am terrified of drowning, the image of being abandoned in dark, icy waters infested with submarines or sharks or anything for that matter is an image that makes my heart race and drops me to my knees in gratitude for the ridiculously blessed life I have.

Recently, I was coming home from a relaxing weekend at my cabin in the mountains. Traffic was unusually backed up on the highway—there was a multiple-car accident up ahead. I could see one car on its side, another upside down, and a third crushed into a shape hard to recognize as a vehicle. After sitting still for fifteen minutes or so, most of us turned off our engines. Some got out to stretch and walk up to see what was going on. The time lengthened into half an hour, then forty-five minutes. I quit looking at my watch after that.

I thought about the people in the accident, about all the heroes helping them, and about other people waiting. Hundreds of us waited. Maybe some were anxious and impatient. Maybe some were worried about being late. Maybe some were angry about being inconvenienced.

But no matter what our feelings were about being stopped, the fact was that none of us were being cut out of our upside-down cars, carefully strapped onto stretchers, and transported to the hospital or the morgue.

After what was, in the big scheme of life, a short time, we all drove past the wreckage and went on with our days.

As we express our gratitude, we must never forget that the highest appreciation is not to utter words, but to live by them.
—JOHN F. KENNEDY

I'm Grateful for That!

After the challenge of forgiveness in the last step, here is a more fun challenge, the gratitude challenge. When you are feeling negative about something, say you are grateful for it. It's okay if you don't mean it. Just say it. Since it is true that we feel the way we act, act the way you want to feel.

I'll give you an example so you can see how it works. Here are the gratitude steps I went through when I was miserably sick in bed for a whole week with the flu:

1. I'm grateful for the flu. (No, I'm not. I'm feeling whiny.)
2. I'm grateful that in the midst of recent stress, my body took charge and ordered me to take a break. (Hawaii would have been nicer.)
3. I'm grateful for the hot tea my daughter made for me. (I haven't coughed in ten seconds.)
4. I'm grateful for the daughter who made it. (My two daughters have been very attentive this week.)
5. I'm grateful for my warm blankets and soft pillows piled high on my bed. (They are comforting.)
6. I'm grateful that I have terrific colleagues who have filled in for me this week while I've been sick. (They are truly the best.)

7. I'm grateful for blog friends and other friends who have sent me get-well thoughts and made me feel cared about. (I have friends all over the world wishing me well.)
8. I'm grateful that I am generally a very healthy person and this is a temporary condition. (I am so lucky to have good health.)
9. I'm grateful to have more blessings that I can even begin to count. (Wow, this really works. I am feeling grateful. How silly to be whiny when I am so abundantly blessed.)

> *The simple exercise of saying "Thank you"*
> *starts a new habit of mind.*
> —PATRICIA RYAN MADSON

On the Lookout for Love

When others offer us gifts of happiness, we might miss them because we are too busy to notice or because we don't think we deserve them. Recognizing and appreciating these gifts will fill up our happiness reservoirs.

Have you ever tried to give a compliment to someone who wouldn't take it? For example, maybe you tell your friend she looks nice, and she responds that her hair looks terrible or she needs to lose weight. Why do we miss these opportunities to soak up the goodness that someone offers us?

Yesterday I decided that I was going to pay attention all day to all the goodness that came my way from whatever source. Here are some highlights:

> When I woke up, my old dog came over to snuggle. I rubbed her soft, deaf ears and thought about all the love she has given me over the years.
>
> I had a long phone visit with a good friend I had not spoken to in a while.
>
> My kids said thank you several times today for various things. It's nice to be appreciated.
>
> A driver made room for me to change lanes.

My sister and I reminisced about some of our best memories of Mom and Dad. I realized how much they did for me out of love. I also felt close to my sister, sharing these memories.

A former student e-mailed to say that something I taught him had come in handy at his job. He wanted to say thanks.

The cashier at the grocery called my attention to some discounts that I had overlooked.

A neighbor smiled and waved.

The sun radiated warmth through the chilly air.

The amazing thing is that at the end of the day, all I could remember was the good stuff. If anything happened that was irritating or upsetting, I didn't notice. My attention was on the positive. I felt blessed.

I'm going to try that again today.

I would maintain that thanks are the highest form of thought, and that gratitude is happiness doubled by wonder.
　　　　　　　　　　　　　　　　　–G. K. CHESTERTON

T-Shirt Wisdom

Spotted on a T-shirt: *NOTE TO SELF: THIS WILL BE AN AWESOME DAY!*

I read an article in *O, the Oprah Magazine,* about awe. Apparently, feeling a sense of awe is good for our health, both physical and emotional. Awe releases feel-good chemicals in our brain that spur us to connect with others. When we experience something that amazes us, our first response is to feel good. Our second response is to want to share it with others. For example, the article said that the most e-mailed *New York Times* articles are not about oil spills and terrorism; the most e-mailed articles are inspirational, like articles about discoveries in space and stories of heroism or courage or generosity.

The article made me realize how often I rush past awe. I don't look up at the stars. I don't pause to delight in the wonder. I don't bother to share my discovery with someone.

So I made a note to myself this morning that it was going to be an awesome day. And I decided to make it an awesome day by trying an exercise I read about in *Roll Around Heaven* by Jessica Maxwell. I'm going to say thank you for everything today. For one day I am going to be grateful for everything, without judgment, without hesitation.

This is how my day has started out:

I'm thankful that...

... I woke up this morning.

... my brain knows where I am.

... I have a cozy bed to wake up in.

... the dog who shares my cozy bed no longer has fleas.

... I can breathe.

... I have eyes that can look out the window at the first faint light.

... I have ears that can hear the construction noise across the street.

... the construction workers waited until I was awake to start work today.

... my house has heat that comes on magically in the morning when I turn the thermostat up.

... I have indoor plumbing.

... I have hot water for a shower.

... my robe is clean and smells good.

... I have my favorite cereal for breakfast.

... I have teeth to eat with.

... I have a computer.

... my computer works.

... (I guess I have to be grateful that my computer is slow as molasses, but I momentarily hesitate on that one.)

That was far as I got when I started writing this morning.

Now I'm going to go be grateful for my toothbrush and toothpaste, and then I'm going to be grateful for my car, which will take me where I want to go. I can't wait to see what will awe me next!

Be grateful for the tiny details of your life and make room for unexpected and beautiful blessings.
–UNKNOWN

Christmas Spiders

When James was three, he helped me decorate the Christmas tree. The next day while he was at preschool, I realized that we had forgotten the tinsel. (This was back in the days before we knew that this was not an environmentally friendly decoration.) I quickly tossed a couple of packages of tinsel on the tree and called it good.

When James came home that afternoon, he went about his business, not really paying attention to the tree. But that evening when he walked into the room after I had turned on the blazing, multicolored tree lights, he froze and stared in wide-eyed amazement at the long silvery streamers glittering in the soft air currents. "Shh. The Christmas spiders have been here," he whispered.

That is a happy memory. This morning I was reminded of it when I encountered several spiders of the summer variety. They seem to be everywhere these days, which is not unusual for Portland. When I woke up, there was one suspended from the ceiling in the middle of my room, floating like a levitating yogi. I got a cup from downstairs, gently scooped the spider, and carried it outside to the garden.

When I opened the car door, there was a perfect web stretching from the steering wheel to the driver's seat. The builder was sitting in the center, ever hopeful in the locked car. I found a piece of paper and, with some regret, destroyed the magnificent creation and carried the spider to the bushes where I thought it would have better luck.

I had driven only a few blocks when I noticed another web connecting the driver's side mirror with the door. The web was already battered by the wind, and the poor little spider was holding on like a bull rider at the rodeo as the web remnants violently vibrated. I tried to ignore it, but after a few more blocks, I sighed and pulled over. I found another scrap of paper in the car, onto which the traumatized little cowboy gratefully clambered. I carried it to the curb and eased it onto a lovely rosebush.

I was briefly annoyed at all the interruptions in my morning, but then I remembered the Christmas spiders. Sometimes when I think back over James's childhood, my heart sinks with memories of all the challenges his autism presented. I forget that there were also magic times of childhood wonder and delight.

Shh. The angel spiders have been here.

Gratitude is the smile of love.
–UNKNOWN

My Plan B Family

My most influential spiritual teachers have been, without a doubt, my children. I have three adopted children and two foster children. All my children, for various reasons, did not end up with their birth families. Being raised by your birth parents is what I would call Plan A. When that doesn't work, then you have to go to Plan B. I am a Plan B parent.

People say to me, "Oh, what a wonderful thing you have done for these children." No, I am the lucky one. My children have been God's greatest gift to me. Each one has given me a gift like no other. On Mother's Day several years ago, I wrote a letter thanking each one.

James gave me the gift of motherhood. The night before he arrived, I kept thinking, *This will be the last night of my life that I am not a mother.* The next day I would become a mother, and I would be a mother for the rest of my life. Being a mother broke open my heart.

Mia gave me the gift of connection. Before her arrival, I lived a very isolated life. But Mia never met a stranger. A trip to the grocery store became a social event. Through her, I became connected to the world around me.

Dan gave me the gift of acceptance. Dan joined our family as a fourteen-year-old autistic teenager. I had to accept him just the way he was. Because of Dan, I learned to accept James's autism as well. And to accept other people, too, just as they are.

Grace gave me the gift of…grace, God's invitation to us to experience unconditional love. To receive God's gift of grace, we must have faith. Faith that God loves us even when others don't or when we can't love ourselves. Faith that God's angels hold us in the light when all we see is darkness. Grace taught me to trust God.

Lily gave me the gift of peace. Her presence radiates serenity and calms the air she moves through. Because she is my last child, my heart feels full and complete. Through Lily, I have learned to rest in God.

To others, my family might appear, well, complicated. When my adopted daughter and my foster daughter both had babies, a friend asked me who I was to these babies. Was I their grandmother? At first I was angry at the question, which seemed at best insensitive, especially with respect to an adopted child, as any adoptive parent can appreciate. Of course I am their grandmother. And yet, I have to admit that the relationships in our family are not always so easy to identify.

For example, my foster son Dan joined our family after his parents died. Although he has been part of our family for twelve years, I have never tried to replace his mother, and he has never called me Mom. But I claim him as my own, and he and James are brothers.

Although I rarely use the labels *adopted* or *foster*, or even think of them, sometimes I do when it seems important to explain the various connections. The kids do the same. For example, Grace will sometimes call me her mom but other times her foster mom, if she is distinguishing me from her birth family, with whom she is still connected. The labels are fluid and used when useful.

But around the table this past Thanksgiving, there were no labels. My heart was full as I looked at all of us: five kids and two grandkids,

Mia's boyfriend, and Grace's dad and two little half-sisters. We all came from different families of origin, different ethnicities, even different countries. Yet there we were, a family, not made by blood but by God, bound not by genes but by love.

Thank you, God, for blessing me with my Plan B family.

> *The family is one of nature's masterpieces.*
> –GEORGE SANTAYANA

Be Glad in It

This is the day the Lord has made.
Let us rejoice and be glad in it.
—Psalm 118:24

My minister often speaks the first sentence of this verse. The congregation responds with the second. It's an automatic response, intoned in unison, without audible enthusiasm or intention. Blah blah blah.

Whatever.

As I listen to the rote repetition of the verse, I imagine thoughts flitting through the minds of those around me: *It's raining outside. My dog is getting old. My spouse doesn't understand me. I have a stack of bills on my desk. I have too much to do and not enough time. The kids are driving me crazy. I'm worried about the stock market. I feel despair about our political climate. And our environmental climate. The birds don't visit my birdfeeders in the garden. A friend isn't returning my calls. I haven't had a vacation in ages. Can't afford one anyway. Dad's mind is slipping.*

I confess that some of these thoughts are occasionally mine. What is there to rejoice about? So I think of another verse in the Bible:

Jesus wept. —John 11:35

I wonder if Jesus weeps when he hears the lack of appreciation for the gift of each day.

When something is automatic, like how we respond to the minister's call, we often overlook it. I rarely, for example, pay attention to my breathing, hearing, seeing. I don't give much thought to the sun's daily circuit, or to the air, or to the lights that turn on at the flip of a switch, or to the water that pours from the faucet, clean enough to drink, hot enough for a comfortable shower.

My daughter and I were sitting at the dining room table having a chat. She was bemoaning certain circumstances, feeling disappointed, frustrated, stuck. I whipped out my handy dandy little pie chart that I use in my discussion group, showing that only 10 percent of our happiness comes from our outer circumstances. The rest comes from inside us. But how, she whined, do you get to that 90 percent when the 10 percent seems like everything?

Indeed. How do we shift our perspective to our inner joy when those outer circumstances are so not to our liking? The key, I think, is in the psalmist's verse.

The first sentence reminds us that every day is a gift from God. The Dalai Lama speaks about the precious gift of this human life. When I wished my friend a happy "special" birthday on his seventieth birthday, he quipped that at his age, every birthday is special. Ask anyone who is dying, or who has been given another chance after a close brush with death, how she feels about each day.

The second sentence begins with, "Let us rejoice." I think of life taking me by the shoulders with a gentle shake and grinning in my face. *Wake up! Pay attention!* This is a new day. How cool is that?!

My favorite part of the verse, though, is the last part, "be glad in it." The verse doesn't tell me to be glad "about it." I don't have to pretend to like circumstances I find unpleasant or distressing. The verse tells me to be glad "in it," in the midst of whatever circumstances I find myself. My gladness is not dependent on the circumstances. My gladness comes from recognizing the treasure I have been blessed with, the miracle of another day.

My daughter was not convinced. How, she asked, could she turn attention away from the situation that she kept obsessing over, that she kept wanting to be different? How could she escape the tyranny of that 10 percent?

I suggested a simple technique I'm sure many of you are familiar with. Can you list, I asked her, five things you are grateful for? As she did, I counted them off on my fingers. Her son, her family, sunshine (a rare sunny winter day in Portland!), going to school, her health. Keep going, I urged. She did. I ran out of fingers and started over. As she hesitated, I started asking questions. Can you see? Can you walk? Do you have a home? Do you have enough food to eat? Do you have clothes? Does anyone love you? Do you love anyone?

After several rounds of fingers, she was smiling. I asked her how she felt when she thought about things to be grateful for. Happy, she said. She paused for a moment and said she didn't think she would dwell anymore on what had been bothering her. She felt ready to move on.

Life is short, as some of us already know all too well, and all of us will learn in time. Every day is a day the Lord has made, the days of pleasure and the days of pain. Let us rejoice in the gift of life and be glad in the blessings each day brings.

Who Found That Parking Place?

This guy is late for an appointment, and he is circling the parking lot along with other drivers trolling for a place, watching for people walking to their cars, trying to anticipate their location and be there first, cursing when he isn't. Finally, he starts praying. "Oh God, please help me find a parking place. If I am late for this appointment, I will catch hell at work. Oops, heck at work. Look, if you will just help me find a parking place, I will go to church every Sunday for a month, I promise. And I'll give a generous donation to the food bank. And I'll..." Just then he turns a corner and there is an empty parking spot right by the front door. "Never mind, God, I found one."

A corny joke, I know, but I laugh every time I hear it, because it reminds me so much of me. I was asked to speak during a church service a few years ago. Sort of a what-the-church-means-to-me kind of testimonial. Even though I often spoke in front of people in my work, this was different. I was very nervous about speaking about my personal life, especially my spiritual life. I thought long and hard. I made lots of notes. I wrote and rewrote. I practiced and practiced again. And I prayed. I prayed more and more as the day approached and by that morning, I was praying nonstop.

"Oh, God, I dedicate this speech to you. I ask you to speak through me and use me as you will. I turn this completely over to you. Whatever happens is as you will, and I accept whatever you want me to do. If this is terrible, then I welcome the lesson in humility. If it is not terrible, then I give all glory to you." And on and on like that. Putting it all on God's shoulders took me off the hook. The moment came. I went to the pulpit and began to speak.

It went well, I could tell. Afterward so many people came up to me to say how much they enjoyed it. Several said I should be a preacher. Seriously. And what was I thinking? *Wow, I was great!* Later, I was embarrassed by how quickly I took credit for success. As quickly, I'm sure, as I would have handed any failure off to God.

I love watching pro football. Now is not the time to get into any deep analysis about why I love it. I bring it up because NFL players are amazing athletes. They train their butts off and play in all kinds of weather and... Well, they are awesome. Sometimes I see a player, after doing something that seems almost superhuman, look skyward and give a quick thumbs-up to God. Or maybe it's a quick thumbs-up to Grandma. Who knows. But it is an acknowledgment of gratitude, a recognition that we all get help along the way.

Feeling gratitude and not expressing it
is like wrapping a present and not giving it.
–WILLIAM ARTHUR WARD

I Love My Life!

I lead a monthly discussion group on the 10 Steps. We focus on one step a month. The most amazing month, I think, is the month we spend on gratitude. For an entire month, I think about gratitude, look for it, write about it, discuss it, read about it, investigate it, explore it, and find it over and over. As I live and breathe gratitude, an amazing thing happens. I fall in love with my life.

Sometimes I will just be going through my day, doing nothing special, and this feeling of sudden, giddy pleasure washes over me. I think, and sometimes even say out loud, "I love my life!"

Sometimes I just shake my head in disbelief at the overwhelming abundance of blessings I have been graced with. My heart swells with such humbling gratitude that I think it might burst wide open like a piñata, and flowers and butterflies will pour forth until the world is covered in them.

That's the best part, really, the way it spills out.

In our discussion group, we spend some time sharing with others what we are grateful for. We realize that we feel happier not only when we tell someone else what we are grateful for but also when we hear what that person is grateful for. Sharing gratitude, whether you are the share-er or the share-ee, increases both people's happiness. We found this to be true even when the listener was not initially feeling very grateful.

Wow, that's something else to be grateful for!

> For each new morning with its light
> For rest and shelter of the night
> For health and food, for love and friends
> For everything Thy goodness sends.
> –RALPH WALDO EMERSON

Our Treasurest Place

My two autistic sons live in a group home for adults with developmental disabilities. It is a modest home by anyone's standards, funded primarily by the residents' government benefits. They do not have lives of privilege or abundance in material things.

I was taking them home once after a family dinner out. As I pulled into their driveway, James said wistfully, "This is the treasurest place on earth." When I asked him what he meant, he paused and nodded thoughtfully. "I have everything I want."

Notice that James didn't just say he has everything he needs. He went further, to say that he has everything he wants. How many of us can say that? How many of us do say it?

Make no mistake, James does want things. A new DVD, a hamburger and fries with root beer, a trip to the library. So what did he really mean? I think he meant that he has everything he wants in order to be happy. I think he recognizes that his happiness is complete whether he has certain "things" or not. His statement was one of utter contentment and appreciation.

May we all live in our treasurest place and have everything we want.

Contentment is natural wealth; luxury is artificial poverty.
—SOCRATES

Butterfly Time

The butterfly counts not months but moments,
and has time enough.
−Rabindranath Tagore

Someone asked me if I have been surprised by anything since I retired. Yes! You'll laugh when I tell you.

I'm surprised that there are still only twenty-four hours in a day.

I thought that when I retired I would have enough time to do all the things I want to do. I thought that the days would stretch invitingly before me with endless hours to fill up with all those things on my when-I-have-more-time-I'm-going-to list. Here are some of the things from that list:

> Learn a new style of martial arts.
> Finish my book.
> Start baking bread again.
> Spend hours puttering around in the garden.
> Spend hours sitting in the garden after I've puttered.
> Read as much as I want to.
> Get serious about learning Chinese.
> Relearn Thai.
> Polish my French.

Learn some other languages I haven't even decided on yet.

Spend more time in meditation every morning.

Write more short pieces for magazines and anthologies.

Keep up with my blog.

Spend more time with friends and with people I hope will become friends.

Cook more often (and better).

Spend more one-on-one time with each of my kids.

Spend as much time as I want with my grandkids.

Stay at the cabin more often and for longer periods.

Be a better blog friend.

Take the dog for more walks.

Drink as much water as I should.

Reconnect with folks I've lost touch with.

Organize and deep clean the house, and keep it clean and organized.

Use more moisturizer.

Did I say read as much as I want to?

And have plenty of time left over to just relax and do nothing.

Yep, I really thought I would have time to do all these things. But I don't. I still have to make choices. I still have to postpone or let go of things I can't fit in. That is just so wrong. I feel cheated.

I heard someone say recently that lack of time was the biggest obstacle to her happiness. I so easily saw myself in her harried exertions, looking for that elusive peace we think more time will bring. But it won't. As long as we think the answer to our happiness is out there, in the ticking of the clock, the sweep of the secondhand, the turning of the calendar page, we will always be chasing the shadow of our joy.

I want to be like a butterfly. I want to shift my perception of time to realize that whatever time I have is perfect. I want to enter into the eternity of every moment, blessed by its beauty, grateful for its gifts, humbled by its grace.

I'm embarrassed by my frantic selfishness in the face of such riches. Time hasn't changed at all. I'm just greedy for more of it. I may not have enough time for all the things on my list, but I'm fortunate to spend the time I have doing what I like to do. Moreover, I have all the time in the world for the only thing that really matters, loving and being loved.

It's enough, after all.

He who knows enough is enough will always have enough.
—TAO TE CHING

Contentment: Priceless

When billionaire John D. Rockefeller was asked how much more money he needed before he would feel satisfied, he famously replied, "Just a little more."

It's no secret that we are a consumer society. You can read all kinds of statistics about how many ads we see, how much we buy, how much we waste. People line up for hours to get the first iPads or the newest iPhones. The Dalai Lama laughs about his love of gadgets. He passed an electronics store every day as he walked to a conference he was attending. By the end of the week, he was full of desire to have gadgets he didn't even know the purpose of!

Our economy depends on our purchases. The wisdom of that is for someone else to debate. But what does it mean for us individually?

Do those purchases bring us happiness? Maybe some do. My cabin in the mountains, for example. I agonized about spending so much money on what was clearly a luxury purchase. Not that the cabin is luxurious (it's not), but it was not a family necessity. Yet over the years, it has been the scene of many happy times, for our family and for the friends we share it with.

But what about all that jewelry in the bank safe deposit box? When I lived in Bangkok, jewelry stores were everywhere, with windows full of sparkling gems and walls dripping with deep yellow gold. I spent a good part of my salary in those stores. I rationalized it by telling myself that it was worth so much more in the United States than what I paid for it. Well, that was true, but so what? Did I sell it and make profit? Do I even wear it? No, it sits safe and undisturbed in the dark at the bank.

In one of my favorite movies, *Harold and Maude*, Harold objects to Maude's habit of just taking whatever suits her needs at the moment—a car, for example. Here is part of the dialogue:

> Harold: You hop in any car you want and just drive off?
>
> Maude: Well, not any car. I like to keep a variety. I'm always looking for the new experience.
>
> Harold: Maybe. Nevertheless, I think you're upsetting people. I don't know if that's right.
>
> Maude: Well, if some people get upset because they feel they have a hold on some things, I'm merely acting as a gentle reminder: here today, gone tomorrow, so don't get attached to things. Now, with that in mind, I'm not against collecting things...

Having things is not the issue. Our attachment to things is what causes us pain. Our hope is that our things will bring us happiness. And that more things will bring us even more happiness. MasterCard ran a series of TV commercials following a general scenario. Someone would be purchasing a series of items, let's say all related to camping. The name and price of each item would flash on the screen. The last scene would show the items being used in some sweet way, like the camping items being used for a father-son fishing trip. Instead of a price, the screen would say something like "Time together before he goes to college: priceless."

If I were in a MasterCard commercial, I would be sitting by the creek at my cabin, watching the bugs skim the water, my dog sniffing around for chipmunks, the sun shining through the mossy, green trees.

The screen would say, "Contentment: priceless."

The most important things in life aren't things.
    −ANTHONY J. D'ANGELO

Step 10

Be Here Now

Be where you are. Otherwise, you will miss your life.
—UNKNOWN

If the present moment is my home, then I spend a lot of time on road trips. Like Dorothy on the wizard's quest, I lie down in the poppy fields of the past, drugged by fantasies of do-overs. I'm snatched up by flying monkeys carrying me into a future fraught with peril. If you knocked my door, you would wait...and wait...until you figured out that no one's home. And yet, like Dorothy, home is really the only place I want to be.

We all know that our minds and attention wander hither and yon, into the past and the future. So in this step, we will develop the habit of returning home to the present moment.

You Are Here

I love maps. I especially love maps that have a little red arrow pointing to a spot that says, *You are here.* You can see maps like that in the mall, on a hiking trail, on a college campus, or even on the back of your hotel room door.

If you look at a map of your life, you will see a little red arrow pointing to the present moment. You are here. Right now. There is no place else you can possibly be. And yet how much effort and energy do we spend trying to be somewhere else? We spend time in the past, longing for better times or imagining endless do-overs of our regrets.

If we are not drifting in the past, we are often anxiously rehearsing the future. Have you ever gotten mad at someone in anticipation of something that you think that person might do or say? I have written in earlier posts about my habit of casting into the future with my "what if" lure. I can spin out scenarios faster than the speed of light. My brain races from one to the next, churning up emotions in reaction to events that have not happened and may never happen. It's exhausting!

Meanwhile, we're missing the only life we really have, this life, right now. We have all read about or known people who have had a brush with death, or who are nearing the end of their lives. What we hear from these people over and over is to treasure this moment, the gift of this breath, the miracle of this instant. And this one.

When death is near, we embrace life, knowing that it is fleeting. We sing with joy, knowing that everything is impermanent. We choose to love, knowing that in doing so, we expose the raw tenderness of our vulnerable hearts.

Open the door of your treasure today, for tomorrow the key will not be in your hands.

—SA'DI

The Good Old Days

W ere they? Good, I mean. My minister this morning spoke of nostalgia at holiday time. A longing for a simpler, happier time. But when were those days? Were they the Ozzie and Harriet days of the forties and fifties? Well, not if you were African American, especially in the segregated South. Not if you were a single mother, whose career opportunities were pretty much limited to being a teacher, a nurse, or a secretary. Not if you lived in a part of the world still reeling from the devastation of war, the lingering effects of nuclear fallout, the hunger of famine, the terror of politically motivated genocide.

Right now, while some folks are yearning for a return to what they recall as a happier time, others are celebrating these days as the good days. Luck changes, tides ebb and flow, fortunes are made and lost. *A Course in Miracles* teaches, "The only wholly true thought we can hold about the past is that it is not here." And yet we spend so much time there, in the past—remembering, reliving, regretting, rewriting, reminiscing. Whether it is a pleasant place to visit or a place of sorrow, we still go there, living in a dream that is gone.

We think the past is set in stone, but how many times has history been rewritten? Not just world or national history—our own history?

I took my mother out to dinner when she visited me when I was living in Paris years ago. I invited some friends whose company I thought she would enjoy, and we went to a very chichi restaurant with a huge window framing the nearby Eiffel Tower. Through the entire meal, as we dined on pigeon (which sounds much fancier in French—I couldn't help wondering if the chef had snatched a few off the windowsill), my mother regaled everyone with tales of my childhood. And while they were entertaining stories (my friends would say hilarious), I kept staring out the window at the dazzlingly illuminated landmark, thinking, *Whose childhood was that?* Certainly not the childhood I remembered, but I could see that my mother believed every word she was saying. I realized that there was not an objective past, but rather two pasts, hers and mine, each vividly real to the one remembering. Let it go. It is not here.

Good old days or bad old days are not today days. So how do we break the grip the past has on us? Gently. By noticing when we are lost in the past, whether in pleasant reverie or painful remorse. By reminding ourselves that our past is a story we tell ourselves, a story we can change or simply drop. By bringing our attention back to the present. Again and again. By practicing until it becomes a habit.

> *Yesterday is history, tomorrow is a mystery, today is*
> *a gift of God, which is why we call it the present.*
> —BIL KEANE

Eternity in a Dewdrop

The only aspect of time that is eternal is now.
—A COURSE IN MIRACLES

I love spending time at my cabin in the mountains. I sleep in a small loft on a mattress on the floor. There is a window right at my head. In the window hangs a prism that, on a sunny morning, scatters tiny rainbows on the pillows and across the sloped ceiling just above my head. They last only a minute or two.

Later, I sit on the deck and watch the sun sparkle in dew dropping from the tips of deep-green pine and fir branches. It looks like forest fairies have tied thousands of diamonds on the trees during the night. As the sun moves and as the breeze whispers, rainbow colors flash here and there.

What an exquisite reminder to be here now. How tempting it is to try to grasp and hold on to this beauty. As the light changes, I move my head just slightly, trying to adjust the angle to prolong the brilliance. Maybe I can sustain it a few more seconds, but suddenly it disappears.

This morning I caught myself thinking about writing about the thrall of the display. How quick I am to start living in the shadow land of "about." *Oh, look how beautiful this is—I can write about it!* And I start writing in my head instead of watching the dew diamonds dance.

Sometimes when I'm meditating, I start thinking about whatever technique I'm using. I start imagining how I would teach someone how to use it. Instead of meditating, I am thinking about meditating. Now that's pathetic. I have to laugh and call myself back to the moment. Attend.

Once in my youthful travels, I visited Banff National Park in British Columbia. In all my travels, I cannot remember any scenery that was more breathtaking than that. I was standing on the side of a mountain looking below me at meadows filled with wildflowers. Across the valley and in the distance, snowcapped peaks cut the horizon as far as I could see. Above me the sky was the clearest, deepest blue you could ever imagine.

And what was I doing? Taking pictures. Suddenly I stopped and realized the futility of my efforts to keep this vista forever. No matter how skilled I was (and I wasn't), no photo could preserve the feel or fragrance of the crisp pure air, or the totality of the scene before my eyes. In my Shambhala meditation training, one contemplation topic is everything is impermanent. Including the past.

Without another thought, I threw my camera off the cliff! (It was a cheap camera, and I was not enlightened enough at that time to think about the environmental faux pas.) I raised my hands to the sky and turned my face to the sun. I took a deep breath and smiled.

I want to live my life, not record it.
−Jacqueline Kennedy Onassis

The Hidden Life of Minds

The author of *The Hidden Life of Dogs* followed her dog around the neighborhood for some months as he went about his doggie business, sniffing, marking, and impregnating. Nowadays you can attach a little digital camera on your dog's or cat's collar and sit in the comfort of your living room watching Fido or Fluffy do what he does. The idea is that by watching them, we can gain some insight into their lives. We can understand them better.

We can do the same with our minds. My mind seems to be busy all the time, but I spend little time really paying attention to what it's up to. So I followed it around for a while — my version of reality TV. This is what I observed:

Mostly, I couldn't keep up. In a very short period of time, I caught my mind rehearsing, reliving, planning, judging, complaining, criticizing, worrying, regretting, thinking, anticipating, wishing, hoping, missing, enjoying, caring. And feeling anxious, content, happy, tired, angry, sad, excited, lonely, resentful, loving.

I did this exercise with the discussion group that I lead on the 10 Steps. As we reported our minds' various wanderings, we were struck by the dissimilarities. Although we were all sitting in the same room, our minds traveled on different planets. In addition to great amusement, we gained much insight into how we uniquely perceive situations and communicate about them.

But I digress. Based on this exercise, I came to some conclusions about my own mind. My mind wastes a lot of time and energy. It does not know how to rest. Harnessing it to focus is understandably challenging. It is like a wild horse. In fact, it is very much like a young horse I once trained. Instead of training the filly to accept a halter and lead when she was very small, I waited until she was an adolescent and very strong, and not at all keen on being directed by anyone else.

Becoming familiar with my mind's favorite pastimes helps me befriend what is uniquely me and helps me train my mind to come home to now.

I wonder what the hidden life of the Dalai Lama's mind is like. Wish I could attach a little video camera and find out!

But I digress.

> *There are only two mistakes one can make*
> *along the road to truth:*
> *not going all the way, and not starting.*
> –UNKNOWN

Awake!

Here is my favorite story about Buddha:

> One day, soon after Buddha's enlightenment, a man saw Buddha walking toward him. The man had not heard of Buddha, but he could see that there was something different about the man who was approaching, so he was moved to ask, "Are you a god?"
> Buddha answered, "No."
> "You're a magician, then? A sorcerer? A wizard?"
> "No."
> "Are you some kind of celestial being? An angel, perhaps?"
> "No."
> "Well, then what are you?"
> The Buddha replied, "I am awake."

Every year I pick a word for the year. It's not a resolution; it's more of a guide word, a reminder word. One year my word was *awake*. Not the adjective, the verb, as in, "Wake up!" Everywhere I looked, my word reminded me to come back from wherever I was and see the world as it really is, as it is right now. I spent decades of my life not seeing the world as it is. Instead, I saw what I wanted to see. I was the diva of denial, the mistress of magical thinking. My life was not real. It was made up, because I was afraid to look at truth. I was living in a dream.

Living in a dream is exhausting. It takes a lot of effort to maintain illusion. You have to be constantly vigilant, on eternal alert to spot and crush any green seedling of truth pushing through the cracks in the concrete. It is not for the faint-hearted.

Some of you might know exactly what I'm saying. The good news, and it is good news, is that eventually we wear out. The strength it takes to hold on to the dream will give out, and we will let go. We will all see the world as it really is, right now. We will, as the Bible promises, know the truth, and the truth will set us free. Even though it might first, as Gloria Steinem promised, piss us off.

> *All things arise and pass away,*
> *but the awakened awake forever.*
> —BUDDHA

Game Change

Life is what happens when you're busy making other plans.
–John Lennon

The term *game change* refers to those moments when a play is made that changes the tide of the game, shifting the momentum from one team to the other, setting the tone for the remainder of time on the clock, foreshadowing victory or defeat. It is a sports term that has become a metaphor for that type of event in many contexts: political campaigns, wars, marriages, careers, and life. It's that moment we remember when everything changed, when the wind shifted, or the sun broke through, or the tsunami hit.

When my son James was in middle school, he was in a special class for kids with developmental disabilities. One Friday after school, when the teacher brought all the kids out to their waiting parents, she came over to speak with me. Her eyes were big and her hands fluttered. She blurted out that a terrible thing was happening to another student. Dan's father had recently died. And now his mother had just been diagnosed with terminal liver cancer. What would happen to Dan? There was no family to take him. Social services was now involved, but there was no foster family qualified to care for him because of his disability. Like James, Dan was autistic.

As she began telling the story, I felt the world shift under me. It seemed like I was inside a tank turret looking through the little rectangular opening when the gears began whirring as the turret turned to aim in a different direction. I didn't want it to turn. I wanted to get James and my daughter and head up to the mountains for a relaxing weekend. I did not want to hear about Dan. In my mind, I covered my ears with my hands and started singing, *La la la, I can't hear you!*

But I did hear, and my life was changed. I wanted my life to go on as it was, but my life could never be as it was, because now I had a choice that was not there moments before. My life was changed no matter what I chose. That moment was a game change.

We went on to our cabin, and I spent the weekend praying. My prayers went something like this: *Dear God, no fair! Please don't ask me to do this. I already have an autistic child. I don't even know Dan. This is not my problem. You are mean. Why are you doing this to me? Please let me walk away.* God just smiled and waited.

And so, on Monday morning, I did one of the craziest things I have ever done. I called the teacher and said I would take Dan. A few days later, I sat down across the table from Dan's mother. A refugee from Vietnam after the war, she had made a life for herself and her family in this country. Her husband was dead, and now she was dying, too. She was bone thin. Her skin and the whites of her eyes were yellow. Her eyes were full of fear.

We had an interpreter, but I didn't need an interpreter to understand her. I understood her better than I understand most people who share my language and culture. I knew that every time she looked at her son, her heart filled up with love beyond measure and broke into a million pieces with grief and worry. I knew that she couldn't sleep at night, terrified about what would happen to her son when she was gone, picturing him all alone in the world with no one to love him or care for him. I knew her like I knew myself. She was living my worst nightmare.

I looked into her desperate eyes and promised I would take care of her son. She cried. I cried, too. She had to trust a stranger with what she loved more than anything in the world. I had to find the inner resources to warrant that trust.

We thought we had a few months to help Dan prepare to transition. The social worker helped us make a plan to begin with some short visits and gradually move to longer and overnight visits. But less than two weeks later, I got a call to pick Dan up from school because his mother had been taken to the hospital for her final hours. So my first experience with Dan was to take him to a dimly lit hospital room, and to stand by his side as he said good-bye to his mother. And then I brought him home. He was fourteen years old and had just lost his whole world.

That first night was chaos. I was not yet prepared for his arrival. I had no bed for him, not even a toothbrush. I didn't know what he would eat. His language skills were very limited. He became frantic and kept trying to tell me something I couldn't understand until he suddenly stood still and I saw the dark spot on the front of his pants and the urine pooling around his feet.

The social worker came over that evening and certified me as a foster parent on an emergency basis. I made a bed for Dan on the floor of James's room. I sat with him and sang lullabies until he fell asleep.

A man's steps are from the Lord;
how then can he understand his way?
—PROVERBS 20:24

Ecstasy in the Laundry

After the Ecstasy, the Laundry is the title of a book by Jack Kornfield. The title reminds us that people climb to mountain summits, but they don't live there. When I fell off the roof of my cabin and had a glimpse of heaven, I still ended up on the ground scraped and bruised. If eternity is in the present moment, is it only in moments of amazing joy? Or in all our other moments as well?

In a TV interview, Denzel Washington told the story of going to visit his mother after winning an Oscar. He was feeling pretty full of himself. He walked in the door expecting her to profess her awe and pride and to treat him like the star he felt himself to be. What did she say? "The trash needs taking out." I love the way he tells this story with a good laugh at himself and affection for a mother who loves him enough to remind him to be humble.

Many of us look for something special. We seek to escape from our everyday lives into spiritual satori. Maybe we only feel connected to the divine if we are in deep meditation, or walking by the ocean, or in an ashram in India. People travel all over the world seeking enlightenment, some evidence of arrival into the promised land. *Yes, I have made it. I am enlightened. See—I can levitate. I know I am saved because I said these words.* Whatever.

If you saw the original movie *The Karate Kid*, you might remember the scene in which the master has agreed to teach the boy martial arts. The boy shows up ready to be initiated into belong to the exclusive ninja club. What does the do? Wax the car. He demonstrates with a cloth in each on. Wax off. Wax on. Wax off." The boy waxes for weeks months, before he gets to do the cool stuff. When he finally gets do the cool stuff, he realizes that what he's doing is exactly what he's already learned. All that waxing *was* the cool stuff.

We sometimes believe that in order to have lives of deep joy, we have to wait. Maybe we have to say X number of prayers, do so many good deeds, read certain books, listen to the right people, attend the class where the teacher has the answer we keep looking for. Or maybe we have to wait for a particular event. We'll be happy when we retire, have a baby, make more money, go on vacation. I don't know about you, but I don't have time to meditate for hours or to turn my life over to a master, no matter how wise. And I don't want to wait for something that may or may not happen in the future. So what hope is there for me?

The good news is that we don't have to do that. Our spiritual practice is what we are doing right now. This is it. I'm sitting here working on my book. Later I will in fact do the laundry. I will take the dog for a walk. I will go to the grocery store. These are not times away from God, away from peace, away from joy. Wherever I am is holy ground. Whatever I am doing is sacred. Holding back and waiting for those "special times" is fantasy. Life is here in this moment. Eternity is here in this moment. Indeed, that is the only place it is.

Wax on. Wax off. Wax on. Wax off.

> *Every now, disappearing just as rapidly as it arrives,*
> *has been shaped and created by a habit and—in its*
> *fleeting existence—is shaping and creating habits.*
> —SYLVIA BOORSTEIN

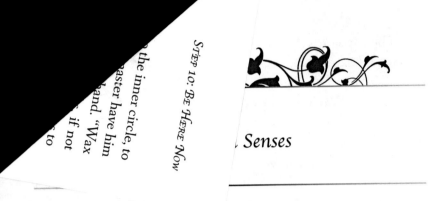

Senses

We carry around with us the key for unlocking the present moment: our senses. When I was a back-to-the-land hippie living in the mountains of Montana with four dogs, I learned a lot from watching them. We would walk and run for miles through the woods. I noticed that while I relied primarily on sight, they used hearing and smell just as much as their sight. They would pause and sniff the wind. I would, too. What did they smell? They would cock their ears and listen. I would, too. What did they hear? They would lick something to see what it was. Okay, I didn't do that!

Most of the time, we operate on automatic pilot with our senses. Our minds wander off until something our senses pick up yanks us back to the present. Soon our minds are off again.

Just like training a puppy to come, we can call our minds back to the present by doing a quick sensory survey.

Try this. Close your eyes and do a quick survey of what your other senses are telling you about the present moment. What do you hear? Listen for a moment. I hear the football game on TV. I hear one of the birds chirping in the kitchen. I hear a humming; maybe that's the refrigerator. I hear the tapping of the computer keys.

What do you smell? I smell my dog lying next to me, in need of a bath. I smell the usual smell of my house, which is hardly noticeable because I am accustomed to it. I don't smell dinner cooking yet.

Taste? My mouth tastes a bit funky since I didn't brush after lunch. There is also a lingering sweetness from the doughnut my daughter brought home for me.

Touch? I feel the weight of my body on the couch. My heel is uncomfortable propped up on the coffee table. My fuzzy socks are soft. My upper body is warm because I'm wearing my favorite sweatshirt. I can feel the weight of the laptop on my legs and the smooth plastic of the computer keys with the little ridges on *F* and *J*.

Having checked in with my other senses, I can now open my eyes and be aware of what they are seeing. My eyes see the computer screen, the dog, the game on TV, the trees outside, the family photos on the mantel, the dog food kibbles on the carpet where Sadie dropped them.

A sensory survey can take less than a minute. It's easy to do while you are at a red light or standing in the checkout line. In addition to bringing us back to the present moment, this technique can also help us calm down when we are anxious or agitated. I'm told that it is also a therapy technique for people suffering from PTSD or panic attacks.

In his book *You Are Here,* Thich Nhat Hanh described a practice called "stopping and deep looking." He suggests that we use a stop sign as a reminder—very practical! We can stop anytime and anywhere, and bring our attention back to the present moment, the only time that is real, the only time we can be truly alive. At least for a nanosecond. I am lucky that I live in a neighborhood with so many stop signs.

> *The source of wisdom is whatever is happening to us*
> *right at this very instant.*
> –PEMA CHÖDRÖN

Training Our Mind Puppy

If you have ever done any meditation, or even just read about it, then you are familiar with the concept of letting your thoughts drift in and out like clouds. In mindfulness meditation, we are taught to focus our attention on our breath and let the thoughts go by without effort—without trying to resist them or hang on to them.

My mind spends a lot of time engaged with its thoughts, in dialogue with endless chatter. "Lost in thought" is an apt description. We all do that. Maybe we are driving along a familiar route and all of a sudden we bring our attention back and wonder where we are. Or we lie in bed at night mulling over things and realize that it is now way past our bedtime and the time left for sleep is short.

I recently read about leave-no-trace camping. As you might guess, the point is to enter and leave the campsite without leaving any evidence that you have been there. This is like mindfulness meditation. Leave-no-trace thinking. Let the thoughts enter and leave the mind without any evidence that they have been there.

Does that mean that thinking is bad? Of course not. I have to think as I'm writing right now, for example. But my thinking is directed and purposeful. It is mindful thinking (in theory, at least). It is different from the hamster-wheel stories that our minds get hooked into as our thoughts wander aimlessly.

I do not spend much time in what anyone would call traditional meditation, mindful or otherwise, although I do meditate for a brief time every morning. But I have been trying to move through my day in a more mindful way. Like the Biblical encouragement to "pray without ceasing," I try to rest my attention continuously in the present.

Sounds good. But do I in fact rest my attention continuously in the present? No. My record is probably something slightly longer than a nanosecond. Father Thomas Keating taught a method of contemplative prayer using a centering word to call your attention back to God. After one prayer session, an exasperated nun approached him and complained, "I am not good at this. I had to use my centering word one thousand times." Father Keating threw his arms up and exclaimed, "That's wonderful! That's one thousand times you were connected to God!"

Our brains generate thoughts. That's what they do. We can't stop that, and we wouldn't want to. But we can keep our mental campsite clean so that the thoughts don't litter the environment. We can let them go, and we can come back to now.

We can train our minds the way we train a puppy, with gentle repetition. We can teach our minds to come when called. And a trained mind, like a trained puppy, is a joy.

Sit! Stay! Heal!
–PEMA CHÖDRÖN

You Have to Be Present to Win

Wherever you are, be all there.
–Jim Rohn

Several people I know died last year. People my age. People who were busy making plans that did not include dying. So, besides missing them, I've had my own mortality in my face, up close and personal. And if I didn't realize it before, I certainly realize now that life is short. While I'm worrying about all the things that might happen in some future I might not even live to see, I'm missing my life right now.

One of my friends who died was Greg. I was shocked when he told me that he had pancreatic cancer that had already metastasized. I didn't see that coming. He didn't either. He looked good and seemed full of vitality. I marveled at his composure and light-heartedness. Every day was a precious gift to him. A day to spend as he pleased, connecting with friends, traveling, enjoying the company of his girlfriend. He was not afraid. He was very much alive.

I spent an afternoon with him near the end. Thanks to the miracle of morphine, he was not in a lot of pain. He was not up and about too much anymore, so we just lay on the bed and chatted. He was very matter-of-fact about what was happening. His body was slowly disappearing. He had always been slim, but by his own description, he was now bony. Auschwitz bony, is what he said.

But he was not morose. On the contrary, we laughed and reminisced about our friendship over the years. He still had a twinkle in his eye and a good sense of humor. I thought about how busy my life was right then with things I thought were so important, so important that I had considered not stopping by that afternoon. I didn't know it then, but that would be the last time I saw Greg. What if I had missed it?

Woody Allen said that 80 percent of success is just showing up. It's like that contest rule, *You have to be present to win.* There is nothing like spending time with a dying friend to remind you about priorities, about living each day like the precious gift that it is, about not wasting time, about showing up, about being present to win.

How much of my life do I miss because I'm simply not there? My friends who died last year gave me many gifts during their lifetimes, but with their deaths they gave me the gift of an intense appreciation for the preciousness of every day.

Our appointment with life takes place in the present moment.
—THICH NHAT HANH

Love Your Death

"Hokahey! Today is a good day to die!" Crazy Horse exhorted his warriors with this cry as they went into battle. (*Hokahey* means something like, "Let's do it!" or "Let's roll!") Were they suicidal? I don't think so.

I don't think the Sioux warriors were seeking death. But they were not afraid of it, either. By living without fear of death, they lived fully. Sure, they died. We all do. But they didn't die in advance, if you know what I mean. Death had no place to enter into their time of living.

Several years ago, my word for the year was *prepare*. The word came to me as I was going through my usual New Year's Eve ritual at my cabin. It was getting close to midnight, and I still didn't have a word that might guide me for the next 365 days. As I was listening to the sound of the creek outside, I heard the word *death*. Hmm, that was not a very happy word, and besides, my word is always a verb. Moments later I heard *prepare*. Well, okay, that was a verb, but not exactly what I was hoping for. How about *enjoy, relax,* or *nap*? But I knew with an inner recognition that *prepare* was my word. As ominous as is sounds, I didn't get the sense that this was any sort of premonition or threat. It seemed more like loving advice. Not a death knell, but rather a wakeup call.

In her last months, as my mom was dying of cancer, we had some wonderful conversations. I asked her questions about her life, like what were her happiest memories, what was she most proud of, what did she regret. Her answers were not the answers I would have predicted, so I discovered things about her that I treasure still. I asked her how she felt about dying, and she responded that she was curious. Curious. Like the French philosopher François Rabelais, who reportedly said on his deathbed, "Je vais chercher un grand peut-être." I go to seek a great perhaps.

Mom was not afraid to die. She was like the monk who stood calmly before the sword-brandishing samurai warrior. The warrior bellowed, "I can run you through without blinking an eye." When the monk replied quietly, "And I can be run through without blinking an eye," the samurai dropped his sword and fell at the feet of the monk, acknowledging his superior power. Mom's ease put me at ease, with death and with her death.

A wise person told me that death is our greatest advisor and our closest friend, because death teaches us how to live. I was sitting by the creek during the summer of the year when my word was *prepare*. Everything was lush and green. The birds were chirping. Everywhere was life abundant. As the sun's warm rays sparkled on the dancing water, I heard the message, *Love your death*. And I understood. Preparing for and loving my death released me from fear. I am free to love my life, to rejoice in the precious gift of each moment.

Every day is a good day to die. Hokahey.

Even death is not to be feared by one who has lived wisely.
—BUDDHA

Be Amazed!

One of my graduate-school professors was from Eastern Europe. He had an often unexpected way of using English. Once he instructed us to turn to a certain page "and be amazed!" I don't remember what was on that page or if I was amazed, but I loved the instruction, and it stayed with me. There is always something new to learn or simply to notice, and it is amazing.

Sometimes I use the instruction on myself. It's a good reminder to look for and see the miracles that are happening all around me all the time. The sun came up this morning. Be amazed. Water came out of the shower head when I turned the handle. Be amazed. It was hot. Be amazed.

It's okay to be amazed with ourselves. I made my bed this morning. Be amazed. I got my black belt in tae kwon do just before my sixtieth birthday. Be very amazed.

Even God amazed himself on occasion. Isaiah 43:19 says, "Behold, I am doing a new thing. Now it springs forth. Do you not see it? I will make a way in the wilderness and rivers in the desert." I love this verse. Like a child delighting in a new accomplishment, God was saying, "Look at what I can do. This is so cool!" I'm no Bible scholar, but I like to think that's what he was saying.

Dream as if you'll live forever. Live as if you'll die today.
–James Dean

Falling into Now

Some years ago, I went to my cabin in the mountains for some quality alone time—no phone, no TV, no kids. Just me and the dog. While I was there, I decided that I needed to clean all the pine needles and debris off the roof. I dismissed any hesitance I felt about doing this task without backup. I used an extension ladder and a long rake. I was cleaning the very last section of the roof when I felt the ladder slip. I frantically clutched at the roof, but there was nothing to hold on to. I knew I was going to fall.

So far, this sounds like any bad accident someone who has no business being on a ladder when no one else is around might have. But here is where it gets interesting. The instant I knew I was going to fall, I let go. I released the fear. Or rather, it released me, since I was not doing it deliberately. (At this point, I was not doing anything deliberately.)

I was conscious as I tumbled. I felt my body bounce off the ladder on the way down. I felt my back hit the edge of the deck, and then I flipped off the deck to the ground below and slid to a stop. But all the way down, I was absolutely certain that everything was exactly the way it should be. I knew that my body might be hurt. I expected that, at the least, something would be broken. Maybe I would be paralyzed or even die. No problem. I knew in my deepest awareness that no matter what happened, no matter how it might seem on the "outside," no matter whether my "normal" awareness could understand, everything was perfect just the way it was.

When I came to a stop, I lay there without moving for a while. The thought crossed my mind that if I tried to move, I might find out that I couldn't. I felt no pain—maybe a bad sign. I wasn't in heaven anymore. I was lying on the side of a hill with my dog. I love my dog, but she is no hero, and I knew I was on my own if I needed help. Finally, I started trying to see what would move. Fingers, toes, arms, legs. I slowly got to my feet, marveling that everything seemed to be intact and functioning (although I was scratched up, bruised, and sore for days after).

I gingerly climbed back up the hill and sat on the deck. My mind started to go to all the scary what-if places. But I stopped. I had been given an exquisite gift. Two gifts, really. First, the experience itself. Second, the memory of it.

In her book *Radical Acceptance*, Tara Brach said, "Radical Acceptance is the willingness to experience ourselves and our life as it is. A moment of Radical Acceptance is a moment of genuine freedom." That's how I felt when I was falling. Genuinely free.

Your journey has molded you for your greater good, and it was exactly what it needed to be. Don't think that you've lost time. It took each and every situation you have encountered to bring you to the now, and now is right on time.

–ASHA TYSON

The 11th Step

You Can Go Home Again

The way is not in the sky.
The way is in the heart.
—BUDDHA

Whither to Now, O Beloved?

Like the impatient children in the backseat on a long drive, we might be asking, "Are we there yet?" And the answer is yes, of course we're here.

Remember when Dorothy returned to Oz to claim her reward for killing the Wicked Witch of the West? Her wish was to return home to Kansas. The wizard promised to take her himself. But after the wizard accidentally flew off in his balloon without Dorothy, Glinda the Good Witch told her she didn't need help to get home, that she always had the power to go home. When Scarecrow protested that Glinda should have told Dorothy that before, Glinda replied that Dorothy would not have believed her—she had to learn it for herself.

Glinda asked Dorothy what she learned. Dorothy replied, "If I ever go looking for my heart's desire again, I won't look any further than my own backyard, because if it isn't there, I never really lost it to begin with."

How far have I traveled all over the world, how many books have I read, how many workshops have I attended, how many times in how many ways have I looked outside myself for the yellow brick road to joy?

Like Dorothy, I guess I had to learn for myself. And what have I learned? That the only place to find happiness is inside myself. Our happy place is not found in a particular lifestyle, diet, feng shui, faith. We can't get there by doing or by going. There is nothing to do and no place to go. Yongey Mingyur Rinpoche says it's like living in a dark room and bumping into furniture until we brush against the switch that has always been right there on the wall and suddenly we see everything so clearly in the light. It's like a fish in the ocean asking where the water is.

Robert Frost said that home is the place where, when you go there, they have to let you in. So I knocked on the door of home. As promised, the door opened, and I found myself where I had been all along. Right here, in this holy instant, in a state of joyful grace.

This book is not about searching. It's about finding, finding our happy place and staying there. Loving ourselves and loving each other. Paying attention to and wallowing in the glory of every moment. Taking a deep breath and experiencing the absolute perfection of, well, everything.

It's about living in the fullness of knowing we are blessed beyond belief. Every day is a gift; everything is a miracle. It's about taking the risk to believe that this is true. It's about stepping through the gate of this holy instant into eternity. To know that we will be changed. Transformed. Into what we've always been.

Thomas Wolfe wrote that we can't go home again. But we can. Indeed, it is the only place we can go because, when we get there, we realize that we never left. We wake up and see that all our wanderings were but a dream.

So come with me. Take my hand, close your eyes, click your heels together three times, and repeat with me, "There's no place like home."

> *And the end of all our exploring*
> *Will be to arrive where we started*
> *And know the place for the first time.*
> —T. S. ELIOT

Further Reading

This is a book born of a blog (10stepstofindingyourhappyplace.com) and retreats and classes I've led. In other words, the book's intended tone is casual and conversational—I write like I talk, which, for a lawyer from the South, means with some level of logic and folksiness. Footnotes would jar us out of the story, and many of the anecdotes I share aren't really citable. They're in the air, long adapted and repeated by many, or retrieved from a memory that is lousy with source details but good with the quote's points. Still, I do want people to be able to find more about the sources I've used. Different voices speak to different people, so I have tried to include a variety. I hope you will find some voices that speak to you.

A Course in Miracles. New York: Viking, 1996.

Baraz, James, and Shoshana Alexander. *Awakening Joy: 10 Steps that Will Put You on the Road to Real Happiness*. New York: Bantam Books, 2010.

Beck, Charlotte Joko. *Everyday Zen*. New York: HarperCollins Publishers, 1998.

Boorstein, Sylvia. *Happiness Is an Inside Job*. New York: Ballantine Books, 2007.

Brach, Tara. *Radical Acceptance: Embracing Your Life with the Heart of a Buddha*. New York: Bantam Dell, 2003.

Brown, Brené. *I Thought It Was Just Me (but It Isn't): Telling the Truth About Perfectionism, Inadequacy and Power*. New York: Gotham Books, 2007.

Chödrön, Pema. *Comfortable with Uncertainty: 108 Teachings on Cultivation Fearlessness and Compassion*. Boston: Shambhala Publications, Inc., 2008.

———. *Taking the Leap: Freeing Ourselves from Old Habits and Fears*. Boston: Shambhala Publications, Inc., 2009.

———. *The Places that Scare You*. Boston: Shambhala Publications, Inc., 2001.

Chopra, Deepak. *The Ultimate Happiness Prescription*. New York: Harmony Books, 2009.

Covey, Stephen. *The 7 Habits of Highly Effective People*. New York: Free Press, 2004.

Dyer, Wayne W. *Inspiration: Your Ultimate Calling*. Carlsbad, CA: Hay House, Inc., 2006.

Ferrini, Paul. *Love Without Conditions: Reflections of the Christ Mind*. Greenfield, MA: Heartways Press, 1994.

————. *The 12 Steps of Forgiveness: A Practical Manual for Moving from Fear to Love.* Brattleboro, VT: Heartways Press, 1991.

Foster, Rick, and Greg Hicks. *How We Choose to Be Happy: The 9 Choices of Extremely Happy People—Their Secrets, Their Stories.* New York: Penguin Group, 1999.

Frankl, Viktor E. *Man's Search for Meaning.* Boston: Beacon Press, 1959.

Hanh, Thich Nhat. *You Are Here.* Boston: Shambhala Publications, Inc., 2001.

His Holiness the Dalai Lama, and Howard C. Cutler. *The Art of Happiness.* New York: Riverhead Books, 1998.

Keating, Thomas. *Open Mind Open Heart: The Contemplative Dimension of the Gospel.* New York: The Continuum International Publishing Group, Inc., 1986.

Kornfield, Jack. *A Path with Heart.* New York: Bantam Books, 1993.

————. *After the Ecstasy, the Laundry.* New York: Bantam Books, 2000.

Kraybill, Donald. *Amish Grace: How Forgiveness Transcended Tragedy.* San Francisco: Jossey-Bass, 2007.

Kurtz, Ernest, and Katherine Ketcham. *The Spirituality of Imperfection.* New York: Bantam Books, 1992.

Kushner, Harold S. *How Good Do We Have to Be? A New Understanding of Guilt and Forgiveness.* Little, Brown and Company, 1996.

Lamott, Anne. *Traveling Mercies: Some Thoughts on Faith.* New York: Anchor Books, 1999.

Lee, Bruce. *Striking Thoughts: Bruce Lee's Wisdom for Daily Living.* Boston: Tuttle Publishing, 2000.

Lyubomirsky, Sonja. *The How of Happiness: A New Approach to Getting the Life You Want.* London, UK: Penguin Books, 2007.

Maxwell, Jessica. *Roll Around Heaven: An All-True Accidental Spiritual Adventure.* New York: Atria Paperback, 2009.

Mingyur, Yongey. *The Joy of Living: Unlocking the Secret & Science of Happiness.* New York: Three Rivers Press, 2007.

Mipham, Sakyong. *Turning the Mind into an Ally.* New York: Riverhead Books, 2003.

Myers, David G. *The Pursuit of Happiness.* New York: HarperCollins, 1992.

Newberry, Tommy. *The 4:8 Principle: The Secret to a Joy-Filled Life.* Madison, GA: The Knight Agency, 2007.

Rubin, Gretchen. *The Happiness Project: Or, Why I Spent a Year Trying to Sing in the Morning, Clean My Closets, Fight Right, Read Aristotle, and Generally Have More Fun.* New York: HarperCollins Publishers, 2009.

Rupp, Joyce. *Open the Door: A Journey to the True Self.* Notre Dame, IN: Sorin Books, 2008.

SARK. *Glad No Matter What: Transforming Loss and Change into Gift and Opportunity.* Novato, CA: New World Library, 2010.

Shimoff, Marci. *Happy for No Reason: 7 Steps to Being Happy from the Inside Out.* New York: Free Press, 2008.

Suzuki, Shunryu. *Zen Mind, Beginner's Mind.* Boston: Shambhala Publications, Inc., 2007.

Trungpa, Chögyam. *Cutting Through Spiritual Materialism.* Boston: Shambhala Publication, Inc., 1973.

———. *Shambhala: The Sacred Path of the Warrior.* Boston: Shambhala Publications, Inc., 1984.

Tsu, Lao. *Tao Te Ching.* New York: Third Vintage Books Edition, 2011.

Tutu, Desmond. *No Future Without Forgiveness.* New York: Doubleday, 1999.

Voskamp, Ann. *One Thousand Gifts.* Grand Rapids, MI: Zondervan, 2010.

Warren, Rick. *God's Power to Change Your Life.* Grand Rapids, MI: Zondervan, 1990.

Weiner, Erik. *The Geography of Bliss.* New York: Hachette Book Group, 2008.

Williamson, Marianne. *A Return to Love: Reflections on the Principles of* A Course in Miracles. New York: HarperCollins, 1993.

About the Author

Galen Pearl's stories have appeared in *Chicken Soup for the Soul* and *A Cup of Comfort* anthologies. Her popular blog, 10 Steps to Finding Your Happy Place (and Staying There), attracts thousands of readers every month. Recently retired from teaching law, she regularly leads retreats and workshops on developing habits to grow a joyful spirit. A Southern girl transplanted to the Pacific Northwest, she enjoys her five kids and two grandchildren, martial arts, her cabin in the mountains, and mahjong.

10stepstofindingyourhappyplace.com

CPSIA information can be obtained
at www.ICGtesting.com
Printed in the USA
FSOW02n0002250516
20776FS